Indonesians in Victoria from the 1950s

edited by
H. Da Costa
J. Penny
D. Anggraeni Fraser

Annual Indonesia Lecture Series No. 19

Based on the 1994 AIA-CSEAS Lecture Series organized by Hilary Da Costa.

National Library of Australia Cataloguing-in-Publication Data:

Indonesians in Victoria from the 1950s.

ISBN 0 7326 0618 7
ISSN 0729 3623

1. Indonesians - Victoria - History. 2. Indonesians - Victoria - Social conditions. I. Da Costa, H. (Hilary). II. Penny, Janet. III. Fraser, D. Anggraeni (Dewi Anggraeni), 1945-. IV. Monash University. Centre of Southeast Asian Studies. (Series: Annual Indonesia lecture series; no. 19.).
305.899220945

Published by
Monash Asia Institute
Monash University
Clayton, Victoria 3168
Australia

Contents

Speakers in Order of Appearance

Dr Janet Penny, Bureau of Immigration and Population Research
Maret Soekotjo, in active retirement
Rudi Munir, Radio Australia
Rabin Hardjadibrata, Monash University
Hugh O'Neill, University of Melbourne
Dr Tuti Gunawan, RMIT University
Hilary Da Costa, AIA of Victoria, Box Hill TAFE
Poedijono, Monash University
Dewi Anggraeni Fraser, Author and journalist
Dr Ailsa (Tommy) Zainu'ddin, Monash Education Faculty, active semi-retirement
Zainu'ddin, in active retirement and constant demand
Dr Karen Sri Kartomi Thomas, University of Melbourne
Zulfikar Alimuddin, RMIT University
Lanita Idrus, Australian Catholic University
Peter Berry, KPMG Peat Marwick

Opening address by Mr Edhimurti Sunoko, Consul of the Republic of Indonesia, Melbourne

It is indeed a great pleasure and honour for me to be asked to open the Annual Indonesia Lecture Series organised by the AIA and CSEAS, Monash University for 1994, and I would like to thank the president of AIA for giving me the opportunity to address the participants this evening.

Glancing through the list of lectures and speakers for the next three weeks, I can see that this series will be very interesting, informative and enlightening, both for the lecturerers and the audience.

The topic 'Indonesians in Victoria from the 1950s' indicates that Indonesian nationals have been residing in Australia, and Victoria in particular, for almost half a century. However, from my own personal observation and from a great number of enquiries through the consulate, it seems that the great majority of Australians still have no clear perception of a country called the Republic of Indonesia.

It is a fact that there are differences between our languages, religions, ethnic composition, population, size and economies, as well as our political, legal and social systems. Nevertheless, both nations, Australia and Indonesia, are in the same geographical region. We have to develop, foster and preserve ways of working together as equals.

In my opinion, we do not have to talk further about these differences but together we should discover the complementary factors that would help us to foster this relationship. In this connection, I am sure that A.I.A., through the leadership of Ibu Hilary, will be able to make a great contribution in fostering a sound relationship between our two countires.

For the majority of Australians who have an average 2.3 children in every family, it would be hard to imagine Indonesia's population of 185 million. With a rate of population growth of 2% annually, it is projected that by the year 2000 and 2005, the country's population will have reached 216 million and 231 million respectively. At this rate, Indonesia is capable of reproducing one Australia every two years.

Time and again we hear that Indonesia is Australia's closest neighbour. The reality is that both governments make efforts to maintain good neighbourly relations. The Australian Government's effort to move closer to Asia, economically, is most welcome. Cooperative ventures would help Indonesia become a 'modern and outward looking country'. Cooperative linkages will benefit both Indonesia and Australia. We have witnessed the good relations between our two governments increase significantly. Therefore, to all Indonesian residents in Victoria, I would suggest that you will continue to be contributing factors, not only to maintain good relations between Australia and Indonesia, but also to further foster friendship by building more bridges of understanding through language, culture and cuisines.

Your presence within the Australian society has made a great impact. You add colour to 'the sunburned country'. With Indonesia's colourful and diverse culture, its music and dances have become part of the Australian multicultural society. The variety of Indonesian cuisines has spiced the taste buds of the Australian people. It is pleasing to see that Bahasa Indonesia has now become a main-stream subject, studied at secondary and tertiary institutions. The language is also taught at primary school level. To all Indonesians who have taken up residency in Victoria, I urge you to spread the positive sides of Indonesia and to appreciate the privileges extended by the host country. I am sure the Indonesian people have become welcome additions to the Australian community in Victoria, and Australia generally.

I sincerely hope that the Annual Indonesia Lecture Series will build further mutual understanding. We in Indonesia are particularly aware that enduring frienship among nations can only be built upon mutual understanding, trust and appreciation. Finally, I would like to reiterate that in dealing with problems arising from our relations, we should always keep in mind that Australia and Indonesia as near neighbours in this dynamic part of the Pacific should not only co-operate, but work closely together in the pursuit of their mutual interests.

Once again, I extend my sincere thanks to the organising committee of the Australian-Indonesian Association of Victoria, and the CSEAS, and to all participants who have made this lecture series possible.

Melbourne, August 1994.

Introduction

Tamu-tamu yang terhormat, Pak Edhi Sunoko, Konsul R.I. di Victoria, Pak Bambang Tarsanto dan Pak John Rumsarwir, Konsul-Konsul Muda, ibu-ibu dan bapak-bapak masyarakat Indonesia dan Australie, selamat datang malam ini. Respected guests, ladies and gentlemen, welcome to the opening night of the nineteenth AILS.

I would like to commence with a quote from JAIA (the journal of the AIA of Victoria) October 1984, written ten years ago by the then editor David Mitchell: 'Every year since 1975, the AIA has cooperated with the Centre of Southeast Asian Studies at Monash University in conducting and publishing a series of lectures. An annual series of public lectures on Indonesia had begun quite a few years earlier than that, as the AIA's solution to the problem of how to celebrate Indonesian Independence Day in the middle of a Melbourne winter. The collaboration with Monash has proved fruitful, with the university providing a regular venue and the facilities for publication and distribution of the lectures. The lectures have been aimed to fit into a rather narrow niche. Since they are to be delivered as public lectures the topic must be something of general interest and they must be clearly presented. In addition, since they must be worthy of publication as academic papers, they also have to be original and carefully considered work. Our lecturers have thus the tricky task of hitting two targets at the same time. On the whole they have succeeded very well, with some hitting bullseyes, some doing better on the one target than another and remarkably few have collapsed crosseyed on the floor of the lecture theatre in the attempt.' It is our fervent hope that this year's offering will not fall flat on its face and that it will, in fact, hit the target.

The list of those early presenters reads like a 'who's who' of the Indonesian-Australian community in Victoria, and indeed Australia: Muhamad Slamet, Ailsa Thomson Zainu'ddin, Margaret Kartomi, Jamie Mackie, Herb Feith, Tuti Gunawan, David Mitchell, Koswara Sumaadjaya, Barbara Hatley, Charles Coppel, Hugh O'Neill and so on. And here they are today: ten, twenty, even thirty years on, the 'founding fathers and mothers', the vanguard then and still showing no signs of becoming the rearguard. Now, in 1995, to these names will be added those of the second generation, some of them the offspring of the founders and others representative of the more recent migrations.

I think most of the audience has some knowledge of the documented facts that 'Indonesians' have been visiting Australia for at least four centuries, in a fascinating and on-going history of trade, settlement, inter-marriage and cross-cultural exchange. Choosing as our starting point the 1950s, a very recent date in the light of four hundred plus years, we are looking at the origins in Victoria of an official, strong, growing and developing pattern of Indonesian immigration as documented by Dr. Janet Penny in her recently completed doctorate. Janet's thesis was the nucleus around which the idea for this year's AILS grew. It is perhaps an appropriate precursor to the celebration of 50 years of Indonesian independence and the 20th anniversary of AILS, both in 1995. This series represents a most sincere tribute to all those who have made up and who continue to constitute, the Indonesian-Australian community, in all its breadth and variety, in Victoria.

How to depict this diversity—what to include, what to omit and who to represent the many facets of the community past, present and future, has been difficult. There are those among us tonight who resisted my blandishments, cajoling, arm twisting and bludgeoning, and those who didn't, thank goodness. And to some of you whose forms of address were at times incorrectly given, please accept my apologies. I trust we've finally got it right.

And now, with very great pleasure, I'd like to introduce Dr. Janet Penny, who is currently working with the Bureau of Immigration and Population Research, and who will set the scene for tonight's speakers.

Chapter I:
Foundations

The Establishment of the Indonesian Community in Victoria

Dr Janet Penny

Background
In the years since Indonesia's independence, relations between Indonesia and Australia have become both closer and more complicated. One aspect which has received very little public attention, and on which this series of lectures will focus, is the growing community of Indonesians who live in Australia.

There are two important reasons for this: the first is that relatively few of Australia's migrants come from Indonesia. I am often asked how many Indonesian migrants now live here. According to my calculations, Indonesian settlers are just over one tenth of one percent of the Australian population, or about 20,000. They are city people—between 85 and 90 percent live in the capital cities—the great majority live in Sydney and Melbourne, but they have not tended to settle close to one another, so they don't form visible communities.

The second reason that this community has not been the focus of public attention is that Indonesians are particularly adaptable people, or as Mr Keating has said, tolerant people. They come from a country with a very long history of multiculturalism.

How do they really feel about living in Australia? The best way to find out is to ask a few Indonesians who live here. In these next three Tuesday evenings we will do just that and at the same time take a historical look at this community. Tonight we begin by looking at its establishment—who were the founding bapaks and ibus, why they came and how they set the tone for the kind of relations Indonesians have had with Australians in Victoria.[1] On the second evening we will see how this community has reached out to connect with the people of Victoria and contribute to the enrichment of Australia's multicultural life. And the third evening will look ahead at future directions for this community, and how it can contribute to realising the best possible relationship between Australia and Indonesia.

Before we focus on the topics for these evenings, however, I want to offer some historical perspective on interaction between people in these two countries. Before the mid-twentieth century, contact was sporadic and involved few people. The extent of contact between people from the Indonesian islands and the Australian aborigines is difficult to know for certain. The story of the trepang gatherers from Makassar is well known, but since no permanent community was established, it does not substantially contribute to our story. Once the Europeans arrived in both of these lands there was some communication by ship, but no substantial trade or contact was developed. There were a few pearlers and a few sugar cane workers from Indonesia who worked in Australia, but few of them stayed on permanently.

For all practical purposes then, the seas between the two countries remained a gulf rather than a conduit for poulation movement. Neither was there much official contact. Before the

1 Because they were well educated—mainly professional—they made a favourable impression on those Australians they met, thus paving the way for others who followed later.

Second World War any official communication between Australia and Indonesia travelled through circuitous diplomatic channels from Canberra to London, to Dutch officials there, and thence to Hague, then to Batavia and back again by the same route. The economies of both countries were set up to serve the needs of the European powers. As a result, there was very little personal, official or trade contact until the upheavals caused by the Second World War.

We will skip the fascinating story of those who came to Australia as employees or as political prisoners of the Netherlands East Indies government, and the sympathy found here for the revolution. However, it is worth noting that as a result of this wartime experience, there developed a core of Australians—particularly in Melbourne and Sydney—who were actively sympathetic to the Revolution. Thess groups formalised as the first Australia-Indonesia Associations of New South Wales and Victoria. The residue of that sympathy was still present when the people arrived who **are** the topic for this evening, those who contributed to the establishment of the Victorian community we know today.

Why did the first Indonesian settlers come to Australia? To begin with, they did **not** come with plans to settle. In the mid-1950s the Australian government had invited three groups of people from Indonesia. First, students were asked to participate in the Colombo Plan scholarship scheme, to help Indonesia develop technical expertise and a system of universities. Second, to present Australia to Indonesia, Radio Australia was established and a few young Indonesians came to Melbourne as broadcasters. And third, experts were invited to teach history, culture and language in Australian universities. There was a fourth group who also helped to form this community—those who came as a result of the Volunteer Graduate Scheme, where young and enthusiastic Australians went to work in Indonesia for a few years. As young people are likely to do, some of them found husbands and wives while on this great adventure, and they, along with a few Indonesian diplomats, joined the others who had been working and studying in Australia.

There is no need to repeat the history of the White Australia policy, but just to emphasise that none of these young Indonesians who were invited expected to stay permanently—nor did most of them want to. While they were pleased to have a chance to further their education to see the world and to earn some foreign currency, most of them fully intended to return and contribute to the development of their new country. Indeed, most of those who came then did return, but there were a few who stayed on.

Why did they stay here? And how did it work out? As the evening progresses their stories will emerge. We will learn how it felt to live in Australia in those days when there were so few Indonesians, or indeed few Asians at all.

According to statistics and the interviews held a few years ago, most of the Indonesians who arrived in the first years have had successful professional careers, mostly in teaching, engineering and journalism. Several of them have become highly respected elders among the Indonesian community and they have also made many close friends among Australians. It can't have been easy in the early years, when Australia was culturally Anglo-Celtic, to have been so clearly different. I hope, as they share their experience with us, it becomes clearer just what it did feel like and what kind of attachments they now have with the country they came from and the country where they have made their lives. Let us begin, then, to hear their stories.

Colombo Plan Scholars

Maret Soekotojo

When we talk about the Colombo Plan we talk about something that took place about forty or so years ago, it is almost like history. Little did we realise at the time that the program could pave the way to gradual change in the way people in this part of the world relate to one another. It was undoubtedly one of the success stories in the Australian Overseas Aid Program. But on a personal level I was just happy to be in it - to be part of it. In fact, I felt fortunate to be selected to come out here and study. But looking back, forty years down the track, I sometimes like to recall the true happiness of how it all started.

It was in late 1954, when I began my second year at the University of Indonesia in Bandung that one day I saw an advertisment in the newspaper. This advertisement was about an announcement of a scholarship offered by the Australian Government under the Colombo Plan. At first I wasn't really interested—you understand—Australia was an unknown quantity because Indonesian education at that time was very much oriented towards Europe. Anyone who went overseas to study most likely either went to Holland or Germany. So I asked myself, 'Shall I put my name on this offer?' I was a little bit unsure that I ought to apply for it. But at the same time I was also aware of what was happening inside the University at that time. There was some sort of unsettled situation, the reason being that that year the Indonesian government has decreed that all lectures in the University has to be given in the Indonesian language, or in English if they wish, but the Dutch language was no longer permitted and in Bandung in the Engineering Faculty most of the teaching staff were still Dutch nationals. That was a problem. Most of them spoke good English but some of their English was only as good as as the students. Communication is difficult when the lecturer is trying to speak in a language that the students do not understand. That was one of the reasons I thought, 'Well, why not?' I wanted to go overseas to study, and that tipped the balance. I forgot Europe and I applied for the scholarship.

A couple of months later I was requested to go through some sort of an aptitude test conducted by what, at that time, was the State Planning Bureau and about six months later I was on my way to Australia. Indonesian bureaucracy was quite efficient in those days. So I became a Colombo Plan Scholar.

I didn't really know how many of us would be going, but before we left we were invited to Jakarta to see President Sukarno. He wanted to send us off with his words of wisdom and it was then that I realised there were about 180 - 200 students going in this program. We were divided into two groups, one going to Melbourne and Adelaide and the other going to Sydney and Brisbane. The first group left in the morning on one plane and the second group left on another plane in the evening. I was in the second group and I ended up in Brisbane, where I spent the next five years. Although this lecture series is mainly looking at the Indonesian population or Indonesian community in Victoria, and my early experience was in Brisbane, I would like to think that similar experiences had happened to students in Melbourne.

The first day when we arrived in Brisbane we were impressed. The place looked clean, tidy and everything seemed to be working quite efficiently. The day we arrived we immediately were given a living allowance and also were divided into groups of two or three, and were allocated accommodation, mostly in flats. Some went into University Colleges. I located a flat in an outer suburb of Brisbane called Corinda. It was the usual large Queensland house subdivided into self-contained flats with the owner or the landlord staying in the same house. There were three of us. The flat was fully furnished, bed linen as well as kitchen equipment—virtually everything was there. The three of us moved in, we looked around and we didn't know what to do. We were young students accustomed to being served all our lives. Suddenly we stood face to face with heaps of kitchen utensils. The reality of what it meant to live in foreign countries started to sink in. We accepted the challenge and discussed it amongst ourselves for two nights.

We were lucky that the landlord was a very helpful sort of person. 'You boys got money?' 'Oh yes, our pockets are full of money. We got it from the Commonwealth'. He took us to the nearest milk bar and he got everything that we wanted, like eggs or oil or whatever we thought we'd need to live. 'Where's the rice?' The milk bar didn't sell rice in those days. There was no rice to be found anywhere and later on I got the impression that no self-respecting Australian would be seen eating rice. Rice could only be purchased at a certain place in Brisbane. We just sort of ate whatever we could get from cans and began to accept the fact that we simply had to adjust ourselves to the new situation.

One of the things we wanted to find out was who else in that city we could talk to, to discuss our problems with, to ask questions. We hoped to find an Indonesian who would talk to us but we found out there was no Indonesian community at that time in Brisbane, however, a few months later we found out that there was one lone Indonesian family, a couple with two young children who were also students. They were the only Indonesian family in Brisbane at that time.

We did ask lots of questions of our landlord, and one day we asked him what we should do with our clothes. You must remember in those days not every household had a washing machine or a car. So we asked what could do we do with our clothes. He said, 'Well, go downstairs, there's a big bowl there, put your clothes in, put soap in there and boil them'. There was a big copper. 'Boil them? How do we boil them?' There was nothing there—you might think there would be some electricity or something to heat it up and boil it but there's nothing there. And we went up stairs again to ask, 'How do we boil it?' 'Go some and get some branches of a tree—start a fire'. That was the way people washed their clothes at the time. Everyone did the same thing. That's how we learned to wash our clothes. That's one of the things I recall of our introduction to life in Australia as a young student.

Apart from the usual University life, we had to attend English tuition classes before we could begin to study. We were all at the stage where we wanted to know as much as we could about the country. But at the same time it became clear to us that this need to learn about one another is not all one way. We found that every one we met was also keen to learn about us Indonesians. Even standing on the platform at the train station was enough for somebody to come to us and ask where we came from, what we were doing here, and that sort of thing. We ended up with conversations at the station, or in a tram or in the street. When buying something, people always asked us, 'Where do you come from?' I got the definite feeling at that time that the Australian public were not yet used to seeing people from Asia in amongst their midst. They wanted to know about us, about why we were here and what we did and that sort of thing.

That need to learn was not only in the street, but also during our stay members of quite a few organizations like the Rotary Club invited us to come to their homes to spend long weekends with them. There must have been quite a number of invitations because everyone got an invitation and during our stay there I received at least three or four invitations to visit Rotary families in places like Toowoomba and Lismore, Kalcoor in northern New South Wales, and they were very keen to know about Indonesia. At that time people knew us as the former Dutch East Indies, even though we preferred to be known as Indonesia.

Also Church organizations invited us to play badminton or tennis for their sports evenings. In those days, the late 1950s, people played more sport than they do today, since there was no television. So there were quite a number of organizations that actually wanted us to feel at home; not only organizations, but also individuals. We knew one lady, a teacher, who was in her fifties. Happily once every month three or four of us always were invited to share an evening with her. Sometimes she invited us for a drive to the sea or the beach. Her house was always full of students; there were also a number of her students from Latvia living at her house. We really felt at home. We needed that, because being in a foreign country as young people we did not really know how to go about approaching people to talk to.

A part of the curriculum in Engineering at that time was the requirement that at the Christmas break we had to spend at least two months working in an engineering plant to get some experience, and we had to find the job ourselves. In those days there was no problem finding jobs. We got two or three offers every year and I liked to come down to Melbourne for job experience. In fact on a few occasions I came down to Melbourne but unfortunately I could see that the students in Melbourne were more fortunate than us because at that time there was an official representative of Indonesia—a Military Attache and an Attache for Trade and Commerce—so the students had somewhere to go, while in Brisbane we had none. In fact at that time the house of the Military Attache was almost like a motel because all the students always went there. In fact when I came down from Brisbane, I had to work in the APM mills somewhere in Gippsland. I stopped and spent the night with them, because they made people feel welcome.

One aspect that arose as a result of living in a different cultural environment is the need to feel secure, the need to belong to something, to belong to a group that one can identify with. That's one of the reasons why in 1956 an Association of Students was formed giving us some sort of a feeling that we belonged to some group of our own, because while we lived in Australian society, among the Australian people, somehow we didn't actually feel a part of it. We kept reminding ourselves that we were here as the guests of the Australian government, as the guests of the Australian people, and that we were here for a temporary stay. While we were aware of what was going round us, and took part in all activities happening around us, we continued to feel we were here as the guests, so we couldn't feel that we were 100% part of the Australian people.

Most of us stayed for five years and so after that the time came when we had to go. When I left Australia I left from Melbourne, not from Sydney or Brisbane because I spent quite a few months in Melbourne before I left. We made a lot of friends here and in contrast to our departure from Jakarta, when everything was official, lots of our friends saw us off. When we left, we had the knowledge that we had made a lot of friends in Australia and also we left with the knowledge that the Australians aren't bad ...

Radio Australia

Rudi Munir

I have been asked to talk about my personal experiences since I came to Australia in 1956, prior to the Melbourne Olympic Games which played a very significant role in all my personal activities, as well as those of Radio Australia. I was working for Radio Republic of Indonesia (RRI) when I was a student at the University of Indonesia. I joined RRI in 1953, I was the national newsreader in Jakarta. Those were very exciting years because we didn't have television then and being a broadcaster from Jakarta was really something because you met important people—celebrities and great singers and in fact, when I was working at RRI in Jakarta I also met my first Australian friends. I met Herbert Feith at the canteen of RRI when he worked as a volunteer with the Department of Information and every lunchtime he came to our canteen. The second person from Australia that I met there was Mrs Molly Bondan, who acted as interpreter with our English Department in Jakarta; there was also a gentleman from Perth, Tom Dimes.

In 1955 when Australia was busy preparing for the Olympic Games, the ABC decided to extend their broadcasts to Indonesia, and other parts of South-east Asia. In the case of Indonesia they extended their time from a half hour to two hours, so they required three new broadcasters from Indonesia. Subsequently they advertised in a Jakarta daily for the first time. Previously whenever they needed new staff they just asked RRI to send somebody as a trainee or exchange broadcaster. But in 1955 when they were planning to extend the broadcasts for the Olympic Games, they put an advertisement in the Jakarta papers and many people applied. I was one of the lucky ones who got the job along with two female colleagues. Well, that was how I got to Radio Australia.

We are talking about the early establishment of the Indonesian community in Victoria. When I arrived here there was no such thing—no organised community as such. At that time there were scores of Colombo Plan students, colleagues of Mas Soekotjo who studied here. There were about ten staff of the Military Attache; Colonel Rokmife Hendraninggrat was the Military Attache and there was a Trade Attache, Mr Gismum Andarisalim, and us at Radio Australia. When I arrived there were two original members, the late Munandar and Azamabdad, and two of my older colleagues from RRI, Ariono Tertohharjo and Abdurahaman, and then we, the three newcomers, making seven in all. So if you would like to call it a community, then that was the community. I think the activities of that community consisted of interaction, interdependence and co-operation between these three groups.

It may sound strange to you that in those years the Military Attache was part of the Embassy in Canberra. The Ambassador, when I first arrived here, was Pak Tamsil, and he had mostly diplomatic staff there. But in Melbourne they needed a spokesman, a public relations person. We at Radio Australia always worked with them in public relations. Every time a VIP arrived from Indonesia who could not speak English but who had to visit industries and things like that, the Attache rang; 'Rudi, could you help?' So we had to go with the gentlemen as an interpreter. Every time there was an official function, national holidays such as Independence

Day and Heroes Day, they always asked us to organize it and we also had to act as Master of Ceremonies and find singers and dancers and organise all that.

But I must say that in those years we ourselves at Radio Australia formed a pool of talent. When we needed someone to appear on television, for instance, we were the first. We appeared in a half-hour program on ABC television presenting Indonesian cultural dancing and singing, together with Colombo Plan students and some members of the Embassy. Mr Ariono, long before Poedijono came onto the Melbourne scene, was the star. He danced all sorts of Javanese stories, sort of derived from the epics—Ramayana, Mahabarata—and everyone recognised him because he is unusually tall for an Indonesian. I am small—Ariono is 6 feet tall. When he wore his Hanoman costume and arrived on the stage he was impressive. So we always worked together.

Another community effort occurred in the late 1980s when the Naval training ship Dewareia arrived in Melbourne. The welcome that the Melburnians afforded them was beyond belief. Thousands of people queued to go on board the ship at the Melbourne Pier, near the Hotel Centra. I went to the ship to interview Commander Rudi Purwano, who later became Admiral Purwano and also the Chief of Naval Operations. Because there were so many people who wanted to visit the ship they needed a PR person. Again, Radio Australia staff were rostered, for morning, afternoon and evening duty, to sit there to take people's names and explain to them the purpose of the ship's visit, where the ship—a barquetine—was built and how long it has been visiting foreign ports. Every mission like that is accompanied by a group of musicians and singers and while they were in Melbourne, we asked the ABC if they would be kind enough to record their music. They obliged so the whole group went into one of the studios at 3LO to be recorded, and we still have a copy of their performance.

There is something else that I don't think many people realise. That small Indonesian community also contributed to the formation of the Islamic Society in Victoria. Our Trade Secretary, Mr Darius Salim, Haji Agus Salim, started the ball rolling by inviting various national groups which included Pakistanis, Malaysians, Lebanese, Turkish and Albanians. In those years there was no mosque. The Turkish community in Melbourne had a house of prayer, which was not a mosque but a Mushollah, a house turned into a mosque and Salim thought an Islamic Society ought to be formed, so he took it upon himself to organise it. We held the Idul Fitri prayers at the Exhibition Building, which we hired for 200 pounds. That was a lot of money in those years but the Exhibition Building is a huge hall. About 600 people came and the idea of forming this organization was put to the meeting and they all said, 'Yes,' so Mr Salim became the President and I was duly elected as the Secretary. Our meetings were held at the Temple Court building in Collins Street because that's where the Indonesian Trade Office was. Salim said, 'Perhaps we'll invite our Ambassador'. At that time Pak Tamil had returned to Indonesia, but Dr Jusef Helmi had replaced him. We asked him if he would be prepared to come down to Melbourne to launch this society and he was very pleased. He came down and on one Abdul Adhar in 1958 the Islamic Society of Victoria was born. Darius Salim and myself were active in that organization for three years but after Mr Salim went back to Indonesia I became involved in other things. I embarked on journalism studies at Melbourne University so our participation began to taper off. But now everybody knows of the Islamic Federation of Victoria with the mosque in Cramer Street, Preston. That was the end result of our efforts back in the late 1950s.

I mentioned earlier about the Colombo Plan students, the Embassy staff and Radio Australia, but when we talk about community we must not forget to include the host families of the Colombo Plan students in Melbourne, because they were particularly active in forming the early community in Melbourne. The AIA was started because the host families, such as Bob and Pat Freestone, launched the idea of forming an association that would help the students to get to know Australia better, to start making friends and also to communicate about culture and many other things. So in 1956 the AIA was formed at Melbourne University. If I am not mistaken the first President was Professor Clarke.The early members, in addition to the host families and some of the students, included the returning volunteer graduates. I also remember that at that time my friend Zainu'ddin began the Indonesian studies course at Melbourne University in 1956.

In 1956 one of my colleagues, the late Abdurrahman, then at Melbourne University where Indonesian studies was very academic, very official, started a casual Indonesian class among friends, among the AIA members, including Don Anderson, Bruce Anderson and Hugh O'Neill and the rest of them. That may have been the beginning of our existing AIA language classes. Those were very interesting years with many activities and we seemed to be doing something all the time. If we were not organising something in Melbourne, there were, as Maret Soekotjo mentioned invitations to speak, I remember I was invited to Moe by the Secretary of the Rotary Club there to give a talk about Indonesia. At that meeting there was another Rotarian from Shepparton who asked me to go there and give a talk. In Shepparton somebody from Wagga Wagga invited us and this continued. But we enjoyed it very, very much.

A number of special events in the early days contributed to our sense of community. The Olympic Games took on great significance for this community. But for the Olympic Games, I wouldn't be here now. That international sporting event provided all sorts of opportunities for Indonesians and Australians to mix. I must also mention again the role the Australian host families played—they organised barbecues every now and then. For example, Bob and Pat Freestone organised the chief barbecue every year at Christmas time at their place in Warrandyte. Literally hundreds of people would turn up. That is just one example. There were also the odd occasions when friends organised barbecues in town at various Australian homes. I think all this contributed to the formation of the Indonesian community. Of course, at that stage, the number of people in this community was small. Everybody was willing to contribute, so everything went smoothly but nowadays, of course, the numbers have grown enormously. I think there are about 8,000 Indonesians now in Victoria, with wide interests, so we don't have that solid community spirit any more, not like when we were small, anyway.

In conclusion, I would just like to mention that in nearly forty years of living in Australia with my Australian family, and also with Indonesian community, many things have changed. As you are all aware there are new generations of Indonesians who have arrived in Australia to study. In those years people came here to pursue tertiary education at Universities, Colleges and other institutions but nowadays many come just to attend high school to get their VCE. When I went to Indonesia I talked to some parents who would like to have their children live with an Australian family, but things are different now. In the old days most students came and stayed with Australian families and learned the Australian ways. They got used to Australian English, but nowadays you need to make an extra effort to be able to live with an Australian family. Nowadays what they call 'homestay' is a nice house organised by the University where students are placed for a few weeks until they enrol. Then they start looking for a flat where they live together. The parents in Indonesia are concerned because these youngsters are not using English. They don't converse in English and they're still speaking in Indonesian after six months of an intensive English course; their English leaves a lot to be desired. These are some of the changes. I don't know how we can improve this, but I suppose if we can put our efforts together we may be able to help these youngsters in the future. Thank you very much.

Academics

Rabin Hardjadibrata

It is always very difficult to talk about your peers, particularly if you are closely connected with each individual person. One can say that the Indonesian academics in Victoria are so closely related that they are almost an inbred group. However, notwithstanding its negative connotation, I'll try to give as objective a view as possible of who the academics are or were and what their contribution have or had been in the advancement of Bahasa Indonesia in Victoria.

The first thing I have to do is to define what it meant by academic. There are many definitions of the word, but the one we are most concerned with here is that of those people who are affiliated with a college or university. The second thing that I have define is the time period under discussion. As we are talking about the establishment of the Indonesian community in Victoria, I have to limit the period to that of 1950-1975, to be precise to the period between 1956-1975. The reasons for choosing this particular period are threefold. First, that it is in 1956 that Indonesian is taught for the first time at a Victorian University, that is at The University of Melbourne, and 1975 is the period where the teaching has expanded not only to Victoria's second university, Monash University in 1964, but also to colleges and schools in Victoria between the late sixties and the early seventies. The third and final matter that needs examining is where the academics are recruited and from what institutions they come.

Everyone knows that reason why—defence, trade and economic reasons aside—Indonesian is chosen to be studied, is because Indonesia is Australia's closest neighbour. It is like the British where they have chosen to study French because France is only across the Channel. Indonesia is just across the Timor sea, it is Australia's closest, most populous neighbour and a culturally diverse country, so if Australia is to get to know Indonesia, they should at least know their language.

Undoubtedly the first pioneer and perhaps the doyen of Indonesian academics in Victoria is Pak Zainu'ddin, who taught full time at the University of Melbourne from March 1956 to December 1960. When he applied for the position he was then a member of the Indonesian Foreign Service and was actually no stranger to Australia as he spent between 1952-1954 in Canberra as a member of the Indonesian Embassy there. He left his full-time position at Melbourne University in 1960 in order to study, although in actual fact he never left teaching altogether, since from 1960 until today he has taught at both Melbourne and Monash Universities part-time.

In 1961 Pieter Sarumpaet took up the post that Pak Zainu'ddin had vacated. He held the position twice, once between 1961-1964, and the second time from 1968 until his death on 19 April, 1991. An alumnus of Universitas Gadjah Mada and Exeter University, in the United Kingdom, he taught at Gadjah Mada until 1960. As an academic he has left a mark in the form of countless publications, both in English and Indonesian, as well as in his mother tongue Toba-Batak. Many of us would be familiar with his *Introduction to Bahasa Indonesia*

(1966) written together with Jamie Mackie; *The Structure of Bahasa Indonesia* (1966); *A Modern Reader in Bahasa Indonesia* (1968) which he co-authored with Hendy Hendrata; *Modern Usage in Bahasa Indonesia* (1980) and an *Advanced English-Indonesian Dictionary* (1994) which was published posthumously. Not listed here are the numerous articles which he wrote during his tenure at Melbourne University.

By 1961 the second university, Monash University, was established. Indonesian/Malay was taught, originally as part of the Department of History, but in 1963 it became the Department of Indonesian and Malay. However, the study of the language Indonesian did not commence until 1964, when I arrived to take up a position in March 1964. The demand for Bahasa Indonesia grew so that in 1965 another lecturer, Iman Partoredjo, was appointed. Both of us, graduates of IKIP Bandung, were at Exeter University between 1958-1960, a year later than Pieter Sarumpaet's group who were there in 1957-1959. I suppose the contribution I made is my research into the frequency of Indonesian words gathered from contemporary Indonesian newspapers, the result of which was partly published in a booklet *Indonesian Morphology, Syntax and Word List* (1980) written together with Bryan Power; and *Sundanese: a Syntactical Analysis* (1985); perhaps an important contribution is my 'opus magnum,' *The Sundanese - English Dictionary,* a comprehensive dictionary of more than 1000 pages, which is almost complete (98% ready). So if anyone knows a publisher, I am open to any offers. When ready this will be the second dictionary of Sudanese-English after 132 years. Iman Partoredjo's contribution is as the two volume editor of Bahasa Indonesia Moderen (1976, 1978). Iman of course, is now teaching as Indonesian Master at the Church of England Grammar school, Brisbane and Tutor at the Institute of Modern Languages, the University of Queensland, Brisbane.

When Pieter Sarumpaet was recalled to Indonesia at the end of 1964, Drs. Supomo Suryohuboyo took up Pieter's position in 1965. Supomo held that position until 1967, when he transferred to the Australian National University in Canberra, where he is until today.

To this time academics appointed to Australian universities were language teachers or linguists. In 1965, Idrus, the author of *Surabaya* (1948) and various other publications such as short stories, was appointed as lecturer and eventually as senior lecturer in literature. He held that position until his death in April 1979 while doing research on the Minangkabau *Kaba* for his Ph.D. In the course of his lecturing he did not forget his creative writing by producing another typical Idrus novel, *Hikayat Puteri Penelope* (1973).

When Supomo left Melbourne University, a vacuum was created in cultural and historical subjects as part of the courses given there. Drs. Muhamad Slamet was then appointed to fill that vacuum. A graduate of anthropology and sociology of non-Western people at Leiden University, before taking up his position he was a member of UNESCO in India. He held the position at Melbourne until the late eighties when he retired. His contributions are a number of articles of a socio-cultural nature, among others 'Let's not crawl back into our shells' in *Indonesian Political Thinking 1945-1965* (1970), 'Priyayi Value Conflict' in *Religion and Social Ethos in Indonesia* (1977), and 'Democratisation and Islam' in *Contemporary Trends in Indonesian Islam* (in print).

One should of course not forget other academics from Melbourne University, such as Hendy Hendrata and Barita Gultom. Hendy was appointed as Senior Tutor in the early sixties and together with Pieter Sarumpaet wrote the best-selling textbook *A Modern Reader in Bahasa Indonesia* mentioned earlier. He left this position to establish the Indonesian section of Victoria College in the late seventies as a lecturer, and eventually as a senior lecturer at the time of his resignation. Apart from his position at Melbourne, he also taught at Monash University's Faculty of Education, being involved in the training of students doing their Diploma of Education. During his teaching Hendy wrote the two-volume textbook based on the very popular Audio-lingual Method, which was then developed into a three-volume textbook entitled An Audio-lingual Course in Bahasa Indonesia. He now runs a successful educational agency. Barita Gultom, on the other hand, worked part-time.

It was during this period, 1968 to be precise, that Indonesian was accepted as an examinable subject, first at leaving and later on at Matriculation level. Most Indonesian academics were at one time or another members of the *Victorian Universities and Schools Examinations Board*, or VUSEB in short, as either Chairman, Deputy Chairman or ordinary members for the Indonesian Standing Committee. As a matter of fact, the syllabus reflects some of the ideas of those academics. It was also at this time that the *Victorian Indonesian Language Teachers' Association* was established; Indonesian academics together with their Australian colleagues were involved in the establishment of VILTA.

By the early seventies three colleges of advanced education begin to teach Indonesian, ie. *Ballarat College of Advanced Education, Bendigo C.A.E.* and *Prahran C.A.E.*. Abe Kelabora was at Bendigo from 1973-1974, before he moved to *La Trobe University* in 1975. His contribution to the teaching of Indonesian can be said to be profound, as not only was he president of VILTA but at a later stage he established the *Indonesian Cultural and Educational Institute* together with myself, with the purpose of promoting the teaching of Indonesian language and culture. A submission to the *Senate Standing Committee on Education and the Arts on the Australian National Language Policy* that Abe and I did in December 1982 no doubt had some influence on the *Asian Studies Council's 'A National Strategy for the Study of Asia in Australia'* published in 1988.

Perhaps another matter that needs mentioning is that it was in this period that a Report, a precursor to the above National Language Policy mentioned above, by the Commonwealth Advisory Committee on the Teaching of Asian Languages and Cultures in Australia (later known as the Auchmuty Report) was published in 1970, in which the Federal Government took a serious interest in Asian Affairs, particularly, with reference to the teaching of Asian Languages and their Cultures. Parts of the report took into account some of the Indonesian academics' submissions. Apart from academic duties, most of us were active in Indonesian Community affairs. Many of us were at one time or another members of the Executive of the AIA; also many of us were the founding fathers of IKAWIRIA 65 and Pieter Sarumpaet and I were the foundation members of the 'Himpunan Pengajar dan Peneliti Indonesia di Australia', HPPIA in short. Perhaps on this note I should end my talk. I have to emphasize that all these facts are based on memory. If there is anything that I have overlooked, please accept my apologies. Thank you.

Volunteer Graduates

Hugh O'Neill

By detaching yourself from the habitual practices of your own culture and becoming lost in Indonesian culture, or in the culture of the group of Indonesians with whom you live and work, you are brought to a deeper understanding of what you really believe in and hold to be important. You do not suspend your critical faculties; yet many of us have found ourselves to be confused in the gap between the two cultures, and some of us have come at times to be very lonely. As we struggle to find our feet in a strange society, it is often difficult to share our deepest concerns with our Indonesian friends, perhaps because so few understand enough of our background. The introspective person, the dreamer, the self-sufficient by nature, has a good start. Nevertheless it will be surprising if, little by little, your love for Indonesia does not grow. In many things you will begin to think like an Indonesian, you will become involved—in part as a sympathetic observer, in part as a participant. This will undoubtedly happen; yet at heart you will remain an Australian.

How would this read in the obverse in describing the experiences of Indonesians coming to Australia?

The statement is paraphrased from the copious briefing documents given to prospective members of the Volunteer Graduate Scheme as it operated from the early 1950s until it was absorbed into the programs of the Overseas Service Bureau about ten years later.

I assume that it reflects something of the preoccupations, even obsessions, of many of us who were lucky enough to be welcomed into the national life of the Indonesian Republic during those heady days, not only as members of the Volunteer Graduate Scheme but many as journalists, academics, Colombo Plan advisers and adventurers.

We will always be grateful for the energetic enthusiasm of friends who laid in the ground work. There is no doubt that they also had a lot to do with the foundation and the remarkable role that the Australian Indonesian Associations have played in broadening the horizons of many Australians.

Although the invitation to us volunteers was to contribute to the infrastructure of Indonesian national development, the central idea was of co-operation and mutual understanding.

The Volunteer Graduate Scheme to Indonesia began in 1950 from the idealism of students and recent graduates at The University of Melbourne. It grew out of the remarkably vibrant student life of that period of post-Second World War regeneration and was facilitated by the community life of organizations such as the AUS, later the National Union of Australian University Students and the Australian Student Christian Movement (ASCM). The program emerged through the extraordinary vision/management abilities and determination of Jim Webb, president of the Student Representative Council in 1952 and later Warden of the

Union at The University of Melbourne. Under his guidance it developed in the early 1960s into the Overseas Service Bureau.

The request from the Indonesians for co-operation and help was made by Aboebakar Loebis at the World University Service Assembly in Bombay in August 1950. It was met with an enthusiastic response from the Australian delegate Alan Hunt, until recently leader of the Liberals in the State Upper House and John Bayly, Melbourne architect and planning consultant, and continued to open up opportunities for Australians to find useful employment in Indonesia.

The hard follow-up work was done by the Melbourne committee Herbert Feith, Betty Evans [later Feith], John Bayly and John and Vernon Bailey and people like Don Anderson and Jim Webb, Chair and Secretary of the subsequent Volunteer Graduate Association.

In 1951 Herb had taken up the invitation made by Loebis and set out under his own steam to work for the Ministry of Information in Jakarta. He was also completing an MA under Professor W. McMahon Ball, of the Political Science Department at Melbourne.

Herb laid the groundwork in Jakarta for the signing of the intergovernmental agreement by respective government ministers in November 1952. I think they were Anwar Tjakroaminoto, Minister of Social Affairs and R.G.Casey, Australian Minister of Foreign Affairs.

Forty *Pegawais* , an acronym for Plan for the Employment of Graduate Australians to Work As Indonesians, were placed during the initial decade. They included agricultural scientists, one architect, economists, engineers, English teachers, librarians, medicos, an occupational therapist, pharmacists, a lawyer,scientists and a social worker.

There were other fascinating links with the Australian-Indonesian communitiy in Australia which helped Herb settle in at the Ministry of Information. Molly Warner of Sydney had fallen in love with Bondan, a pre-war fighter for Indonesian independence and one of the political prisoners held at Boven Digul. He had been repatriated to Australia by the Netherlands Indies Government in exile. Molly had followed Bondan to the revolutionary capital, Yogyakarta, a few years before Herb arrived and was now working as a journalist in the Information Ministry. She and Bondan were friends and counsellors to us all.

An anecdote: The last word of my briefing from Mr Sam Dimmick, the Australian Cultural Attache as I arrived in Jakarta in mid 1958, was 'We don't want you to have anything to do with Molly Bondan'. That was when President Sukarno was working through his programme of Guided Democracy. Fortunately I really couldn't **not** accept her previous invitation to lunch the next Sunday. I had just been down to Pasar Baru to purchase my beautiful new black Australian Government issue bicycle and was feeling as free as a bird. After Sam's warning I wasn't at all surprised when Molly invited me to stroll in her beautiful garden after a delicious meal and reminded me that the peasants of Asia had paid for the industrial revolution. And then she took me to a neighbour's wedding party where I saw my first Wayang. She was still offering her generous hospitality in the late 1980s and continued to write speeches for the Foreign Minister at the same time as advising former Melbournian

Helen Jessup in research for her exhibition and publication *Court Arts of Indonesia* for the Festival of Indonesia in the USA.
Subsequently the Volunteer Graduate Association helped in focussing similar moves in Britain and the USA. Committee members were invited to Washington to consult President Kennedy's advisers in establishing the Peace Corps; not that the Australians thought that the Americans got it right!

Two years ago there was a delightful reunion between Aboebakar Loebis, Feith, Hunt and Bayly at the Fitzroy national office of the Overseas Service Bureau while Pak Loebis was attending the Indonesian Democracy Conference at Monash University. In 1950 he had come to Bombay from Burma where he was the Indonesian Revolutionary Government representative. The fact that the Monash conference was mounted in recognition of Herb Feith's contribution to international understanding of Indonesian political events of the 1950s, made the reunion very special.

The Overseas Service Bureau which carries on the programme in the 1990s, now responds to requests from governments and community based organizations in 40 countries of Africa, Asia and the Pacific. This year it will have interviewed several thousand applicants and recruited more than 400 people to work for two year periods in a wide range of areas of development assistance.

A fortnight ago I spent the evening with about 60 of these people at a briefing at St Mary's College in Parkville. Among them was a Chilean born, Melbourne trained architect setting out for Managua, with her two children and partner. Her ambition is to contribute to education and development of the built environment in Nicaragua; her partner will keep the household going at the same time as continuing his community support work begun in Melbourne's west. Another woman I chatted with is a social worker back for a week between stints with an NGO working in the field of HIV control in Madras. Others were going to countries of Africa, to Vietnam and China.

The Indonesia program is burgeoning—there are about 30 in the field at the moment—no doubt reflecting a determination by Australians to grapple with the realities of the Australia-Indonesia relationship. A young environmentalist will work in Samarinda with an NGO. She will assist in research to regulate timber regeneration in East Kalimantan. A young couple with a family are setting out for two years in Padang to teach research techniques in the field of anthropology at Universitas Andalas .A computer programmer will spend a couple of years at Rantepao, Tana Toraja, in a secondary school; and two English teachers will work as pegawai negeri in government departments in Jakarta. Francis Riggs has just left for Yogya to follow up co-operative work with the Rape Crisis Centre there which has been under way for almost a decade.

'Yet at heart you will remain an Australian,' the 1950s briefing document reminds us. Many of us will sense the tensions arising from moving across national boundaries, and the stimulus and excitement we can get from discovering another culture—and it can go on seemingly for ever.

The cross-cultural dimension of the volunteering experience keeps on surfacing most persistently. The fourth objective of the Overseas Service Bureau, reformulated in 1990 as we re-examined directions, is that the Bureau 'will use the knowledge and experience gained by returned volunteers and others engaged in overseas development programs to increase public awareness of aid, development and cross-cultural issues, both in Australia and overseas. The people-to-people relationships symbolised so succinctly by the Australian-Indonesian Association, and its activities, also characterise the close relationship between the volunteer experience and the AIA co-sponsoring this forum.

A principal motive for young Australians going to Indonesia forty years ago was to try to comprehend our own place and culture by being useful in the process of building amidst another place and culture. It certainly opened up intriguing vistas which continue to expand. In those early years the A.I.A. reflected many facets of friendships between Australians and Indonesians who were fascinated by each other's spirit of nationalism. The early shared experiences of soldiers and political activists in both countries and the determination of the founders of the volunteer movement sparked a bond of mutual understanding and internationalism which made the Australian-Indonesian Association in Victoria a unique organization. It became the forerunner of other friendship societies which followed, as educational and economic links began to develop between Indonesia and Australia in the 1960s, and has continued to do so to the present day.

Chapter II:
Reaching Out

Introduction

Hugh O'Neill

Last week we heard some very interesting tales, principally about what it was like come to Australia many years ago and we heard about the reactions of a student who came and studied and went home and then came back again and has been contributing a lot, with his wife to the life of the Indonesian community and the Australian-Indonesian community. Rudi, not quite the Doyen perhaps but almost, of the Indonesian community, his extraordinary story of being employed in Australia to communicate a lot, with his wife again, as very much part of the Australian Indonesian community.

Rabin Hardjadibrata represented the academic employment scene in Victoria and he has had a long career in teaching and publishing, contributed an enormous amount to the development of studies in Indonesia, particularly through language, and of course made his own very special contribution by giving this opportunity which is about to happen to study his own West Javanese language. I was in a somewhat difficult position because I had to reverse the tale a little, but I suppose it might have helped to give an impression what it was like to go the other way, and of course it was very much conditioned by more recent years with living together in what must be I think the most remarkable cross-cultural experience in the Victorian community, but maybe I'm wrong. It always struck me that the Australian Indonesian community in Victoria was somehow very special, probably because it was crossing such remarkable cultural barriers. Indeed that was the experience that we all had when we went off to Indonesia and as we still do have of course to visit a culture which is so remarkably different from our own. And as everybody has picked up of course and will continue tonight to pick up, the extraordinary richness and passion that is associated with that cross-cultural experience.

So tonight we have four speakers who are going to tell us about the way in which the Indonesian community reaches out in the Victorian community—has reached out and continues to reach out, and next week will be about prognosis and the future. For me—I'm a bit too young to be writing on that very early experience but it was very important to me in the early '60s when I returned from Indonesia, having spent six months working in London, which was the kind of prescribed thing for the professional architect to do. It was professional suicide for you to go to Indonesia in 1958 and it was said, 'Why aren't you going to London or to America to entrench your experience in architecture?' They said, 'You are doing no good!' So I went to England very reluctantly via Japan, Cambodia, Thailand, India and places like the Mediterranean, and spent six months working with a firm which had been focussing on this part of the world. Maxwell Fry and Jane Drew were a very well known firm that set up the tropical school of architecture and for some reason they ran it over the winter period. Freezing in London alongside me were some Nigerians and some Malaysians, some Indians and Pakistanis, learning how you do tropical architecture! A funny idea—but they were interesting people and they had very interesting projects and they were very happy to have me on board, so it wasn't professional suicide at all. I went to the office of employment at the Architectural Association in London and within half an hour I was being interviewed by the most famous woman architect in the world, Jane Drew, and the next day I was in employment, so it wasn't really at all professional suicide to say the least.

But all the time I was in London I drove people mad because I talked about Indonesia all the time. In those days in the late '50s and early 60's, Australians were hanging around London as Humphreys has dramatised so frequently, boring everybody with stories about 'Down Under', but they thought I was a bit screwy because all the time I talked about Indonesia. On the way back I only reinforced those impressions.

But in the early '60s it was my wont, and I discovered this wonderful film, made 'Indonesia Calling', which you got by going down to the Waterside Workers Federation building in Flinders Street. I would walk into the office and they would say, 'Oh, you're here again to get that film are you? In the steel filing cabinet there.' It was a marvellous film which really has immortalised the relationship which developed between Indonesians and Australians during the '40s. The extraordinary Dutch film maker captured all the drama of the relationship which existed between the former political prisoners and the Australian waterside workers; and it is still a great film, of course. It was a kind of surreptitious thing going to the Waterside Workers Union, and then you would take it back and they would put it back in the steel cabinet, until next time.

Then in the early '70s I got a phone call from Canberra, from Foreign Affairs. They said, 'I hear you know about this film 'Indonesia Calling''. You can't imagine what it was like because of all the ups and downs, as I mentioned last week, of the Australian/Indonesian relationship over the previous 10 years. Foreign Affairs said, 'Do you know where we can get a copy of 'Indonesia Calling'?' I said, 'What do you want with it ?' They said, 'To show them in Djakarta'. It was quite an astonishing kind of reversal of the situation it seemed to me and so I said, 'You can get it from the Waterside Workers Federation'. But now, of course, it is in the archives in Canberra and is their fundamental document about Australia/Indonesia.

But of course that wasn't the beginning of it all, those wonderful warm days that we will hear about tonight I am sure of the coming together of Australians and Indonesian in that immediate post-war revolutionary period. There were before the war other sorts of contacts which one rarely hears about. The traffic in bananas between Java and Australia and (I am not quite sure of the dates but I think) the Fijian bananas were starting to come in about 1928, but before that all the bananas to Australia came from Banongya. When I went to Bandung, walking around the streets of Bandung in the '50s there were big horses and they said, 'That's good Australia' and I said 'Why good Australia—that's a strange name?' They said, 'Oh, they all come from Australia'. How they got there I'm not sure, but somebody was telling me a story the other day about the horse racing interests and of course that was revived later on in the 70s, wasn't it, when those 5 or 6 millionaires from Melbourne got together, led by the Taranto millionaire—Taranto icecream—and they took jumbo jets full of race horses to Djakarta and set up the whole racing thing and they thought they were going to make a lot of money; but they had no idea how subtle and complex those people in Djakarta were in laying their bets. They didn't have to go through any kind of turnstile at all, they found their way through the barriers some other way so nobody made much money out of it all.

But one night I was in Djakarta and happened to fall into the company of these millionaires and we were having dinner somewhere in Thamrin in the days when bacaks still went up and down Thamrin. They were staying at the Hotel Thamrin and so they decided to have a race down Thamrin in the middle of the night in the becaks and so they were laying bets on becaks running the Thamrin—it was quite exciting I must say.

But of course it goes further back than that and I doubt whether we will be dealing much with the extraordinary and fascinating contacts that Australians had with Indonesians before the Europeans came to Australia and it has always been of great interest to me and I have never been able to follow it up. But a friend of mine, who is the head of the Batchelor College just outside of Darwin in the Northern Territory, told me about the projects they had had with the Aboriginal people who studied at Batchelor College going off to Makassar and meeting up with the descendants and families of the aboriginal people who had gone back with the traders.

Tonight we have four very interesting people to speak—Tuti Mitchell, Hilary Da Costa, Poedijono and Dewi Anggraeni Fraser: and the first is Tuti Mitchell—Dr Mitchell is Graduate of Anthropology from the University of Indonesia and also a doctor from Monash University, and she comes from a most distinguished and eccentric family I know from personal experience, having met her first, I think, at her wedding to David in Djakarta. So Tuti will speak to us tonight about the community organizations. She has been, on and off, since the late '60s most active in the community organizations in the Indonesian community in Melbourne. So Dr Tuti Mitchell, or Dr Tuti Gunawan should I say, either way, we welcome you tonight.

Indonesian Community Organizations

Tuti Gunawan

I shall start where the previous speakers left off last week, when they spoke about the foundation years.

Sooner or later a migrant community will find a need to form an association, not only to find ways of handing down its culture and language, but also to find solutions to its common problems. The Indonesian students set up their association in the early days of 1955, the Persatuan Pelajar Indonesia or PPI. Ten years later, in 1965, a community organization was set up, named Ikatan Warga Indonesia di Victoria (Indonesian Community Association of Victoria) or IKAWIRIA, with the encouragement of the Indonesian Embassy. It was set up with members of the three components of Indonesian community at that time: students, Indonesians working at Radio Australia, and academics working on contracts with the University of Melbourne - altogether the number did not exceed a few dozen. In these early days only Indonesian citizens were members of the organization and it was conceived more as a way for the Indonesian community to keep in touch with the Indonesian Embassy, rather than to deal with problems in the community, because there seemed to be very few problems of a social nature that were experienced by the community at that time. Perhaps because of its limited scope, the association languished after a few years and was disbanded in 1969.

Thus when I first came to Melbourne, it was the AIA that I was introduced to, and my first involvement with organizational work in Melbourne was with the AIA; I was a member of the committee when AIA under Hugh O`Neill's presidency gave its first winter lecture, in Doncaster Shopping Town, with Dr David Penny, the late husband of Janet Penny, as the speaker.

IKAWIRIA was revived again in 1973 in essentially the same form, except that now Indonesians who had taken up Australian citizenship could also become active members and office holders of the association.

Meanwhile, the Indonesian community had undergone substantial changes. In the 60s the community was small; everyone knew one another. It was a cosy, tightly-knit community. In the 70s, a number of students and other members of the community married Australians and decided to stay here, some because it was difficult for foreign spouses to become permanent residents of Indonesia. There were also Australians who had been to Indonesia and married Indonesians and brought their spouses here. These families and their children made the community in Melbourne more varied and more colourful, (pun intended).

The wider Australian community had also changed. The 'White Australia' policy was officially abandoned in 1972. For this we should pay tribute to the work of the 'Immigration Reform Group', several of whose members were Australians active in the Australian-Indonesian community, such as (now Prof. Emeritus) Jamie Mackie and Don Anderson. This change allowed many people who were other than those allowed by the Migration Act of 1958 to come to Australia.[2] A few years later, an easy visa system was also introduced. Thus while in the 60s and early 70s the community was homogeneous, middle class and educated, consisting of people who came to Australia either as students, as contract lecturers or broadcasters and the like, by the late 70s and 80s a new element had arrived: young people who came to Australia under their own steam, to seek a better life, as either legal or illegal. migrants. Many of them found employment in the manufacturing sector. After the Regularisation of Status (better known as the 'Amnesty') in 1981, most of them became permanent residents, adding yet another ingredient in the enrichment of the community.

By the 1980s there were changes in attitudes, too. In the 60s and early 70s most Indonesians who came here saw living in Australia as a temporary state. They wished to go back to Indonesia into the fold of the extended family when they became old, and to die there. They saw themselves as guests in a foreign country. Consequently few took up Australian citizenship, and few were interested in taking part in the wider Australian community activities other than their own work-related organizations. Thus the activities of the community of Indonesians as seen in the activities of PPI and IKAWIRIA at that time were celebrations of important Indonesian national days such as the Independence Day celebration, the Idul Fitri and Hari Kartini. It was an inward-looking and very nationalistic community. People who took up Australian citizenship were regarded with disapproval. But by the 1980s Indonesians began to regard Australia as a place where they would spend their old age and as the place where they would be buried when they died. With this came the realistic appraisal of the situation, of the demands of career, etc. Many took up Australian citizenship.

In Indonesia the New Order government was consolidating its position. It promoted the Indonesian State Philosophy, Pancasila, as the safeguard against the extremes of the left, that is communism, and the extremes of the right, factions who wanted an Islamic State. Perhaps because of this there came a letter to the Committee of IKAWIRIA, arguing that as an organization with Pancasila as its base, it shouldn't have on its committee people who had taken up Australian citizenship.

I gathered from members of the IKAWIRIA committee at that time, that this letter caused an extensive soul-searching among the committee. It had been in 1973, five years previously, that IKAWIRIA allowed members who had taken Australian citizenship to have full rights in IKAWIRIA, and the subsequent strong growth of IKAWIRIA testified to the richness of the talents drawn from various sectors of the community, which, although still small, nevertheless was growing. To limit membership only to Indonesian citizens would restrict its vitality. The committee also noted that there would be increasing numbers of Indonesians who had taken up Australian citizenship who were gaining good positions in the civil service or in semi-government corporations. Their accumulated knowledge was vital to the smooth transition of many newcomers from Indonesia into settling in to Victoria. It concluded that it was unwise for the long-term growth of the community to alienate these members by barring them from membership or from holding committee positions, as would be the case in an organization

2 The Migration Act of 1958 only provided 'for the temporary admission of non-Europeans who are highly qualified or of special distinction or who are merchants, students, tourists, etc.'

which, by having Pancasila as its base, was potentially putting itself under the political control of Indonesia. The IKAWIRIA then decided in its General Meeting of June 1979 to modify its Constitution and used *'Kekeluargaan'* as its base, rather than *'Pancasila'*, as it believed that 'Kekeluargaan' implies *gotong royong* or mutual help, which is regarded as the essence of the Indonesian spirit and social philosophy without the political overtones of Pancasila. Thus it tried to reconcile the various members, Indonesian citizens, Indonesian-born Australian citizens, and their Australian spouses.

Not all Indonesians saw it this way, however; some saw IKAWIRIA as being disloyal to Indonesia. Some of these people and others, for other reasons, in July 1981 set up another organization, IKAWIRIA '65, based on Pancasila and in which only Indonesian citizens are allowed to be full members.

The use of the splinter organization of the name 'IKAWIRIA'[3] caused a bitter split in the Indonesian community. Its allegation that IKAWIRIA was anti-Pancasila brought an atmosphere of fear among many Indonesians who then withdrew from organizational life altogether, paralysing the community. The unpleasant atmosphere **concerned** many Australians who felt that their Indonesian spouses were put under political pressure and there were those who objected to IKAWIRIA '65 continuing to use the name 'IKAWIRIA' when it was already a registered name[4]. It caused some serious rethinking about the nature of the community. Is it an Indonesian community under the umbrella of the Indonesian State, just as say the Pramuka or Golkar[5]? Or is it a community of people of Indonesian background, united by a common bond of common residence and being in the same country, Australia, no matter what their nationality or religion. Those of the second opinion tend to quote an Indonesian *proverb 'Di mana bumi dipijak, di situ langit dijunjung'*, meaning that where one find one's livelihood, that is the country one must support. It does not have to extend to relinquishing one's citizenship, but it does mean that one should contribute to that country and to obey its rules and laws.

The debate about the nature of IKAWIRIA also goes along these lines: Is it an expatriate organization, that is, an organization of Indonesians who are temporarily out of Indonesia, or an ethnic organization for those Indonesians and also for their children and grandchildren? Citizenship is not easily transferable to the next generation. Children of Indonesians are Indonesian citizens only if both their parents are Indonesian citizens, or at least if their fathers are Indonesian citizens. By Indonesian law, children of marriages of Indonesian women with Australian men cannot become Indonesian citizens. On the other hand, children of

---

3 It is not an uncommon practice in Indonesia that a splinter group takes the name of the group it leaves. An example is PNI (Partai Nasional Indonesia, the Indonesian Nationalist Party) in 1966, which split into 'PNI Osa-Usep' and 'PNI Ali-Surachman'. The strategy behind this is that the splinter group hopes to push the original group out of circulation, or, if or when it fails, that the government would determine which group it favors. The same strategy seemed to be used in Victoria, with IKAWIRIA '65 claiming it had the support of the Indonesian Embassy. An Embassy official was present at the formation of IKAWIRIA '65.

4 Letter of 10 Australians to the President of IKAWIRIA '65, 17 December 1983.

5 Pramuka is the name of the scouting movement in Indonesia; Golkar or Golongan Karya is a 'functional group' formed towards the end of Sukarno's presidency and later became one of three sanctioned political parties.

Indonesians, where one or both parents are Indonesian, can obtain Australian citizenship easily if their parents are residents of Australia. Thus it was inevitable that the Indonesian community would contain many more Australian citizens than Indonesian citizens. IKAWIRIA saw itself as an organization for the whole community of Indonesians present and future, for the present Indonesians and their children, not only for those who are Indonesian citizens. IKAWIRIA '65 saw itself as an organization under the umbrella of the Indonesia State (*'organisasi yang berkiblat ke Indonesia'*), and derisively called IKAWIRIA *'IKAWIRIA etnik'* (ethnic IKAWIRIA) to distinguish it from IKAWIRIA '65.[6]

IKAWIRIA '65 changed its name to PERWIRA (Perhimpunan Warga Indonesia di Victoria) in September 1984[7]. PERWIRA's community activities also include holding Lebaran celebrations, fairs, picnics and community activities. It too sees increasing numbers of its members adopting Australian citizenship, so that it can be envisaged that it will face the same dilemma faced by IKAWIRIA two decades earlier: the need to accommodate adjustments to life in Australia and maintaining adherence to the (Indonesian) state philosophy. Subsequently PERWIRA has people of Australian citizenship as members and committee members, although its Constitution technically still limits full membership to Indonesian citizens.

As I have mentioned before, with the changes in the composition of the Indonesian community, there are new challenges faced by it. Although Indonesians on the whole adjust very well to life in Australia and unemployment is low among Indonesians, some problems do exist. There are Indonesians, mostly women, who came as spouses and find the cold weather and the isolation caused by language problems hard to bear. Then there are people who want to sponsor family members. While in the early days individual members took it upon themselves to help in these cases, increasingly the community as well as government departments look to Indonesian community groups for assistance, informally or formally.

This has further convinced many Indonesians that they cannot just live here and keep behaving like visitors. To be able to take charge of their own affairs, they have to take part in the wider community, and cannot always rely on the Embassy or people from other ethnic groups to look after their affairs. Thus in 1983 IKAWIRIA joined the Ethnic Communities' Council, the only Indonesian community organization to do so, and when the 'Blainey Debate' on Asian immigration broke out in 1984, IKAWIRIA was one of the founding members of a pan-Asian ethnic organizations, now called the Asian-Australian Resource Centre. With these steps, the Indonesian community through IKAWIRIA has reached out not only to the wider Indonesia-related Australian community, but to the wider Australian community as well. It took part in the campaign to protest the Australian Federal

6 However, in 1984 PERWIRA (the name IKAWIRIA '65 adopted in 1984, see below) registered itself under the (Australian) Association Act 1979, thus strictly speaking becoming an organization under the law of the Commonwealth of Australia.

7 The name was suggested by PWNI to the Indonesian Consul at the time (letter of the PWNI Committee to the Indonesian Consul, Mr Kuncoro Pranoto, ...198 ..). PWNI or Persatuan Warga Negara Indonesia was an organization of Indonesian citizens set up as a reaction to the existence of IKAWIRIA '65. It was worried that the antagonistic nature of the setting up of IKAWIRIA '65 was detrimental to the relation between Indonesians and Australians in Victoria. It disbanded itself in March 1988, when the PIA (Persatuan Indonesia di Australia) was formed.

government's plan to abolish SBS-TV. In 1987 it applied and succeeded in getting funding in the Community Employment Program, a Federal Government's program to help long-term unemployed to find jobs. The people employed under this program subsequently succeeded in getting full time employment. Another step is the active participation of the community in setting up the Ethnic Public Radio 3ZZZ, as it had done previously in 1976 with the establishment of Radio 3EA.

A change in attitude occurred also in the field of gender. Women had always been important in the community, but in the organizations of the 1970s they took charge of positions seen to be 'especially suited' to females, such as the women's section *(Seksi Wanita)*, food coordination section (*Seksi Konsumsi*), and occasionally as Treasurer or Secretary[8]. The positions of President and Vice-Presidents were always held by males. This changed in 1982, when I was elected President of IKAWIRIA. Subsequently women have become Presidents and Vice-Presidents in IKAWIRIA, AIA and student organizations.

The late 80s and early 90s also saw the proliferation of other organizations of a specific nature, sometimes as an effort to bridge the gap created by the conflict between IKAWIRIA and PERWIRA. The Islamic Study Group was formed, to be followed by other Islam-oriented organizations in later years. The Islamic Study Group, although set up by Indonesian Muslims, deliberately did not use the word 'Indonesian' in its name to avoid having to deal with Pancasila. The Protestant and Catholic members of the community also set up worship oriented groups, firstly with the establishment of the Indonesian Christian Fellowship, and later with the establishment of groups affiliated with mainstream Australian churches such as the Catholic Church, Uniting Church, the Baptist Church, etc. Within the Christian community a similar dilemma as faced by the members of the general community, also occurs. Here the question is: do we want an Indonesian church, under the umbrella of the Indonesian Council of Churches, or a church which happens to use the Indonesian language in its liturgy, but is under the umbrella of an Australian mainstream church or denomination? This dilemma is still being debated at present.

Interestingly this dilemma does not beset the Islamic organizations, perhaps because in their gatherings there are a large number of Muslims from Malaysia who take part. The same cannot be said about the Christian organizations.

Mention must be made of the Paguyuban Jawi or Javanese Speaking Society whose membership consists of Indonesians and Australians who want to practise speaking Javanese as a cultural pursuit. It has succeeded in avoiding the pitfall of '*sukuisme*' or ethnocentrism by opening its membership to anyone interested in Javanese culture, not just to Javanese. Melbourne is different in this regard from Sydney where associations based on Indonesian ethnic groupings abound: the Batak group, the Minang group, the Kawanua (as people from North Sulawesi call each other) group , etc.

8 With the exception of PPI (the student association) of Victoria, which had a female engineering student as its President in 1973.

There are also other groups which are less formal such as the *arisan*[9] groups, soccer and music groups. The Sekolah Indonesia was formed at the initiative of IKAWIRIA but later became a separate organization.

In the meantime Indonesia has changed too. Economic development in Indonesia has brought self-confidence and a more relaxed attitude among Indonesians in Indonesia towards outsiders. Consequently the need to be defensive and its flip side, to regard people from other countries in a hostile light, has less urgency. Representatives of the Indonesian government in Australia presently put less emphasis on the distinction between 'us' (Indonesian citizens) and 'them' (Australians and Indonesians who have adopted Australian citizenship) and instead put more emphasis on trade and good relations between the two countries. From this point of view all sections of the Indonesian-Australian community are potentially helpful in increasing trade between the two countries. They have also seen the potential benefit in getting help and advice from Indonesians or descendants of Indonesians who are conversant with the ways of Australian society. Indonesians in Indonesia themselves are getting used to the idea of Indonesians working in other countries such as the Middle East, Malaysia, Brunei etc., and of the foreign exchange that these activities can bring. People who do *merantau* find that they do not have to justify themselves for doing so and for taking up another country's citizenship; economic necessity and the idea of accumulating experience are reason enough.

The Indonesian Embassy has initiated the establishment of several organizations: the Perhimpunan Indonesia di Australia (PIA), partly as an effort to heal the rift in the Indonesian community, and the Dharma Wanita, an organization of wives of civil servants, as a branch of Dharma Wanita in Indonesia.

Increasingly, migrants see benefits in becoming Australian citizens. While previously there was almost no reason to take up Australian citizenship unless you wished to become a civil servant or to advance in one's work in a semi-governmental body, now there are tangible avantages in becoming an Australian citizen. Indonesians find it easier to take up Australian citizenship. Another tangible advantage is the introduction of the points rule in immigration procedures, that is, a potential migrant would get an extra 5 points if the sponsor is an Australian citizen. In 1992 and again in 1994 the Australian government mounted a campaign to encourage migrants to take up Australian citizenship. Although I do not have the facts to say how successful is the drive among Indonesians, I think that this, combined with the changes outlined above, have encouraged more Indonesians to take up Australian citizenship and thus alter further the face of the Indonesian community in Victoria. In conclusion I see the development of the Indonesian community and its organizations as reflecting and reacting to changes that have happened in Australian society, such as the abandonment of the White Australia Policy and further adoption of multiculturalism, as well as changes in Indonesian society.

---

9 *Arisan* is characteristically a women only meeting, usually held once a month in a member's home. Each member contributes the same amount of money, e.g. $25 or $100 each month. In each meeting members draw a lot; the winner collects the whole contribution of that month which she spends on a big item such as a refrigerator or a holiday. Members see it as enforced saving (without interest) of money which would otherwise be frittered away; some see it as a way of being in touch once a month with their friends.

AIA of Victoria

Hilary Da Costa

To embrace the history of the present AIA of Victoria in 20 minutes, placing emphasis on the period from the late 1960s to the late 1970s, will not enable full justice to be done to its fascinating past or to the many people who contributed to it. Also, I am mindful that in terms of time I am a 'Johnny-come-lately': there are many in the audience tonight who are able to speak with far more authority than I because they were actually there both before, during and after the period in question. However, since I am 'it' at the moment, and my attempts at delegation failed on this score, I will try to give you a simplified history.

I have attempted to give the picture as accurately as possible by speaking with as many of the 'founding mothers and fathers' and their successors as possible, not only recently, but over the ten years I've been associated with AIA, and also by reading the publicly accessible material in the forms of old files, newsletters and, in particular, early copies of JAIA, the annual Journal of the Australian-Indonesian Association. I am not blessed with the best of memories for facts, like some people I know and envy, so that if anything I present tonight is incorrect I will expect those in the audience, of whom there are many as I said, to correct or amend what I say. And, if in presenting any facts I inadvertently cause offence, please forgive me.

To briefly set the scene, I would like to draw on Margaret Kartomi's research into the first AIA—the Australia-Indonesia Association (Victoria Branch): please note the name—it combines the names of the two countries, and refers to Victoria as a branch, and this is significant as you will see later. It was formed in August 1945, at the time of the declaration of Indonesian independence, by Indonesian nationals resident in Melbourne. I quote Margaret from the Silver Jubilee edition of JAIA of August 1981, exactly 13 years ago, edited by Hidris Kartomi who was AIA president at the time, and Joe Coman of Radio Australia. '...The present-day AIA, constituted in 1956, had a predecessor in the second half of the 'forties'....with stated aims very similar to those of the present AIA, but......with a rather different character and type of membership, especially when compared with those of the 'seventies'.' Beginning in 1945 this AIA had 26 members in 1947 according to the 1947 files, which were apparently the only ones in existence when Margaret did her research. Margaret says this AIA 'was essentially a radical organization, active at a time when racism was blatant in Australia and Indonesians were fighting a four year war against the Dutch' and 'was the more politically motivated' of two groups formed when some members broke away in 1946 to form the East-West Committee: the AIA devoted itself to Indonesia whereas the East-West Committee aimed to help various Asian national groups. AIA's stated aim was 'to help foster friendship and cultural relations between our two peoples.' However, Margaret says,'....a reading of the files suggests that a more precise aim of the AIA was to assist Indonesians in their anti-colonial struggle. As this aim was achieved in 1949 and Indonesians were gradually repatriated, there was no longer an urgent need for the association to exist and so it did not survive into the 'fifties'.' Leading figures in the 'forties were Mrs Jean Zakaria, the

Australian wife of one of the Tanah Merah prisoners, Jack Zakaria, and Jim Cairns, then a lecturer at Melbourne University. Interestingly, and as a sideline, a letter was written to the Melbourne 'Age' newspaper on 21st.July this year by Nooraya Zakaria, daughter of Jack Zakaria . But that is another story and I musn't get sidetracked. Thus Margaret writes, 'Although there is in many ways a vast difference between the activities of the present AIA (ie. that of the 70s and early 80s) and its predecessor, these were dictated by the times.'

Which brings us to the 'fifties', to the time of the re-born and re-constituted AIA, and that of last week's speakers. The re-emergence of an AIA was indeed 'dictated by the times' and was stimulated, as you heard last week, by the presence in Melbourne of Colombo Plan students from Indonesia, University teachers, Radio Australia personnel and the earliest Volunteer Graduates, Herb Feith being the formative figure of the last-named group. From the horse's mouth—sorry, mouths—those of Ailsa and Din Zainu'ddin, I learned of the present AIA's beginnings. From letters, other documents and their recollections, the facts emerged that the present AIA began its new life in August 1956—7th August to be precise. There were six signatories to its formation including Don Anderson, Jim Webb, Zainu'ddin himself and Pat Freestone, names that appear time and again. The first president was Professor Max Clark of Melbourne University and the name adopted by the organization, after much discussion was the Australian-Indonesian Association of Victoria. Well, what's in a name? A lot! In rejecting the names of the countries and opting for the adjectives describing their citizens—Australian and Indonesian—the focus was switched from a politically oriented country to country relationship to that of person-to-person. This reincarnation was to be involved in social support networks and at its inaugural meeting at Melba Hall resolved to form an association with the aim of 'fostering and promoting friendship, understanding and good relations between the peoples of Australia and Indonesia.' To this day, this aim remains. The AIA of the 'fifties' and 'sixties' concentrated on offering friendship to Indonesians in Melbourne and in facilitating the mutual exchange of knowledge about the two countries and their peoples. Barbecues, parties, outings, and cultural performances to celebrate Independence Day kept the growing group busy and united. Names like Pat and Bob Freestone, Vern and Ethel White, Don and Joan Anderson and Ailsa and Din Zainu'ddin appear time and again in the archives. A language class under the late Abdurrachman of Radio Australia began, as did a fund-raising auxiliary, a private hospitality scheme was in place, cultural exchanges were planned, talks and small exhibitions for country areas mooted and a small Indonesian cookbook was published: the little book grew into a bigger book in 1965 and 'How to Cook Indonesian Food' by A.G.T. Zainu'ddin remains in print today and continues to sell. Membership stood at 220 in 1960 and 213 in 1961, its maximum since inception.

As the 'sixties' progressed more well-known names appear: the Fiddians, the Kartomis, the Slamets and the Abbas family. Many famous Indonesian names appear in the annals of the association as 'visitors' and 'visited'. The period of Konfrontasi saw a downturn in membership but by the late'sixties' and early 'seventies' membership was on the rise again. Presidents Lambert, Zainu'ddin, Mackie, White, O'Neill and Travers presided over this period from 1960 to 1974.

The 'fifties' were a growth period and the 'sixties' one of consolidation: the 'seventies' showed another growth spurt possibly reflecting the interest aroused by the visit of President and Ibu Soeharto to Melbourne, the increasing strength of the Indonesian language and studies departments at Monash, Melbourne, and Latrobe universities and the slowly but steadily increasing numbers of Indonesian visitors and settlers. This last phenomenon also led to changes in the composition of membership of AIA as the Indonesian community began to form its own groups in response to the needs of its members as an expatriate community. To quote Hidris Kartomi in his president's address in the formerly mentioned JAIA of 1981, 'over the years (late 60s and 70s) other organizations with basically similar aims have come into being and the AIA has welcomed them and cooperated with them. These days, most of AIA's activities involve cooperation with these many sister groups—PPI, IKAWIRIA, IAS, VILTA, Balinese Dance Society......Indeed, many AIA members are also members of one or more of these other organizations.' This was true of then as it is today. The 'seventies' saw the strong re-emergence of Indonesian language classes with such names as John Collins, Hugh O'Neill, Cathy Mardisiswoyo and the Handfields. Cathy has told me of the initiative of Philip Jones and others in holding highly entertaining debates in Bahasa Indonesia. One of the 'sister' groups referred to in 1981 by Dris was the IAS—the Indonesian Arts Society—the 'brain-child' of Hugh O'Neill and a group of Indonesianists with a strong interest in Indonesian artistic and creative expression. Original members of this group were academics, returned Volunteer Graduates, gallery owners, students and travellers who shared this interest. The society began in 1974 and continues to reach out, inform, educate and entertain. The AILS began, known as the Winter Lecture Series, a cooperative venture of the AIA and the CSEAS at Monash.

Pak Poedijono arrived to take up a teaching position in the Music Department at Monash, to help initiate a flowering of Indonesian performing arts in music, dance and wayang. All these activities within the multi-faceted Indonesian-Australian community began to be reflected to the wider community and indicated a growing strength and confidence, and a desire to inform. Maybe because of the emergence of all these varied interest groups, particularly those initiated by the Indonesian community, the membership of AIA had once again gone into a decline by the early 'eighties'. It seemed that maybe the flowering of interest in educational areas for Bahasa Indonesia had lost some of its momentum and the tourism push to Indonesia was only just beginning.

AIA celebrated its Silver Jubilee in 1981 with the handsome, erudite and absorbing JAIA referred to earlier. Many of AIA's newer members at this time appeared to be students, graduates and researchers based at Monash which retained its enviable reputation as a centre of Indonesian language, studies, and research, but a devoted core of the original members remained as ever faithful to the aims and brief of AIA and carried it through the relatively leaner times again. JAIA, to me, looking back at the changing 'shape' of AIA over the years, reflects very much the presence of academics and teachers, and those with a keen interest and extensive knowledge, of Indonesian culture. JAIA very much represents a confident 'reaching out' to the community in a desire to share this interest and knowledge. Maret Soekotjo, Nuim Khaiyath, Bill Fiddian, David Mitchell, Ketha Carter and Richard Mathews are names that appeared regularly.

This brings us the the last ten years of AIA, 1984-1994, about which I feel I can speak a little more confidently and authoritatively than the previous periods. Membership has grown from around 100 to more than 500 and creeps up each month.

During this period AIA has consolidated its educational and cultural brief through its language classes which now run for 35 weeks each year across 6 levels using experienced and highly-qualified and mainly native-speaking teachers. Our third Summer Intensive Language Course will take place in January 1995. The courses have grown to meet the demand of the teaching and wider community. AIA has also offered English language assistance to Indonesian post-graduates during this period and has helped to network many private language-teaching situations.

The 'AIA News' has also grown to meet the demand and growing interest in Indonesia of the community. More than 500 copies are mailed each month some interstate and overseas. JAIA re-appeared in the late 80s and is now a regular, annual publication that, since 1992, incorporates contributions from the sibling organizations in NSW and ACT.

Socially, Malam Ngobrol, held on the last Friday of each month, provides a relaxed setting for Indonesians and Australians to practise their language skills whilst sharing friendship and developing a deeper understanding of each other's cultures. The popularity of Malam Ngobrol, coupled with the increasing numbers of Indonesians studying and visiting Victoria, is causing us to consider venues other than private homes, most of which are not equipped to contain 70 or more guests! AIA shares in many activities with the Indonesian community organizations in a spirit of cooperation, support , networking and friendship.

A further reaching out , this time between the two countries, took place in the 'mid-eighties' when AIA provided financial support for a project in Central Java to provide desperately needed water for the village of Baturetno. It was felt that some of the accumulated funds should be used to support some grass-roots, self-help or 'bottom up' assistance, to use the popular jargon, in Indonesia. Following Baturetno, in additon to an on-going commitment to Foster Parents Plan Indonesia (now Plan International), using the contacts and expertise of committee, members and interested outside professionals several other schemes have been possible and reached successful conclusions. These have included two three-month training schemes at the Macfarlane Burnet Research Centre, Fairfield and the Royal Children's Hospital for an Indonesian microbiologist and a paediatrician respectively, smaller support for a village and leper hospital in West Kalimantan, financial assistance in South Jakarta for a scholarship scheme to enable children from a very poor kampung to carry on their schooling and financial assistance for an Islamic orphanage in the same area. Other schemes are under consideration for the future.

As in the past, from the inception of AIA, all this has been carried out in a voluntary capacity by dedicated committees. Perhaps this minute is appropriate to make public recognition of their vision and dedicated contribution to furthering the Australian-Indonesian relationship as a voluntary, community-based, interest group. Thank you all, past and present.

And what of the future? In the current climate AIA will doubtless continue to flourish, grow and change shape subtlely in response to the times and the character of its committee and membership. More has been left out tonight than included, and one day, in the not too distant future, I hope a comprehensive history will be written of this unique association as testimony to its colourful history and characters. It has been for me a great pleasure and privilege to be a part of AIA, and I shall step down in October with a mixture of sadness and relief. As my good friend Din , in his wisdom and experience, said to my husband recently, 'Behind every good woman there's a man'.

I'd like to thank Ken, and Rachel and Cathy, without whose support I wouldn't have been able to enjoy myself so much!

Performing Arts and Music in Victoria

Poedijono

I first came to Victoria at the beginning of the 1970s at the invitation of the Monash Music Department, under a three month contract. Interest in Indonesian language and cultural studies was growing in strength and the Music Department wished to offer studies in aspects of Indonesian music.

There were 24 music students interested in studying gamelan at that time. In order to teach them, a gamelan was borrowed from the Indonesian Embassy in Canberra by the Music Department and after one month's instruction and practice, I decided that we were ready to perform. I had brought only two sets of costumes with me from Indonesia- Gatutkoco and Topeng Tua. However, I discovered that a few of my friends in Melbourne owned some wayang puppets; wayang from Solo, Yogya and Bali, and even some wayang golek. I began to form ideas for the performance.

In a gamelan performance there are usually dancers. Fortunately, at this time, I became aware of the presence in Melbourne of mbak Cathy Mardisiswoyo who became the dancer in my concert about Gatutkoco Kromo. In the concert, the Gatutkoco dance was from Java, the Abiosonya (Gatutkoco's grandfather) dance from Bali and the Dewi Pergiwo dance from Solo. The wayang was a combination of Yogya and Solo styles. This first concert, which involved five performances, attracted more than 2000 people, including students, the general public and the Indonesian Ambassador who travelled from Canberra. After this I returned to Bali, Indonesia, where I worked as a teacher at the School of Music.

The following year I received a second invitation from Monash University Music Department. It seemed, as a result of the success of that first concert, the department was in a position to purchase a gamelan. In 1973, with assistance from my family in Wonogiri, this was accomplished. It was with the Monash gamelan that I was later able to choreograph Sendratari based on stories from the Ramayana and Mahabarata legends. This was accomplished with help and donations from the department, students, teachers and the community.

Actually, long before this time, there had already been gamelan performances in Melbourne. At the Hotel Metropole and at Monash, the iron gamelan that was made by Indonesian political prisoners in Digul, Irian Jaya, had been played publicly. It had been brought to Melbourne in 1940 by Mr.Bei Ponco Pangrawit. Also, there was a calung Sunda group brought to Australia under the leadership of Mr.Koswara of Radio Australia. But, it was between 1975 and 1980, that Indonesian musical performances reached a maximum.

In 1975 the first gamelan tour of country Victoria took place. Fifteen music students went by bus to Geelong, Castlemaine, Swan Hill, Manangatang and Mildura where they were warmly received by the public and especially by school children. In 1977 a group toured Canberra,

Tasmania and Armidale, NSW. In 1978, for a period of a week, the gamelan toured Adelaide and surrounding areas. These performances incorporated gamelan, wayang and dance. Many invitations were received as interest grew.

As a result of the interest in Indonesian culture, a number of cultural groups formed such as Sekawari (Balinese Dance Society), Pusaka Nusantara (Kroncong) and also Hidang (Hawthorn Indonesian Dance Group). As the 1980s progressed, a number of gamelan ensembles were purchased. After the Monash gamelan came Scotch College, the Victorian College of the Arts, Deakin University and the Music Department of New England University in Armidale. Sekawari also owned half a Balinese gamelan. In 1989, Flinders University in South Australia purchased a gamelan and also erected a pendopo for performances. Melbourne University, on the other hand, bought three types of gamelan including a Sundanese gamelan degung. The Indonesian Consulate acquired a gamelan at Pak Edhi's initiative. Even primary schools were becoming interested: primary schools on the Gold Coast, at Castlemaine and Grovedale near Geelong, now own sets of gamelan instruments to aid in teaching Indonesian music and culture to students and teachers.

Throughout the 1980s and the 1990s there have been some marvellous concerts and performances of a variety of Indonesian regional dances, drama, music and shadow puppetry. The growing numbers of Indonesian students studying at tertiary institutions are very active in promoting their cultures and many of them are talented and accomplished performers. Gamelan, angklung, traditional dance and drama, as well as modern dramas are staged by the various Indonesian departments at universities, tertiary and secondary colleges. Annual performances, not only to celebrate Independence Day, have become a feature of the Indonesian-Australian community. Fairs, bazaars, trade promotions and so forth provide venues for the Indonesian community to display its culture through music and handicrafts.

The Indonesian Arts Society, which has a long history in Melbourne, has held three significant public exhibitions of textiles, musical instruments and masks respectively, which also raised public awareness of the diversity of Indonesian arts and culture. The AIA has also supported many artistic endeavours and works cooperatively with the Indonesian community.

Invitations are received regularly from schools all over Melbourne, and the state, which are teaching Bahasa Indonesia. The gamelan and wayang kulit are increasingly effective in raising interest in Indonesian arts among students and the school communities. Often these schools use stories from the Ramayana and Mahabarata as teaching materials.

Today, gamelan orchestras are played regularly by several community groups at Monash University, Melbourne University, Castlemaine and at the Indonesian Consulate (by a group of AIA members).

From small beginnings an awareness of several Indonesian music, dance and drama forms has grown in the wider Australian community, supported and promoted by the Indonesian community and Australian schools and universities. Books, videos, documentaries and films are more available and accessible to reinforce and extend cultural awareness. More and more

Australians are visiting Indonesia and returning to Australia wanting to keep up their interest in the culture and language of Indonesia.

I have been very happy to play a role as a performer, teacher and ambassador for the performing and musical arts of Indonesia in Victoria over the last twenty years. I look forward to maintaining an active role in this area for many years to come.

Literature and the Press

Dewi Anggraeni Fraser

A community which lives outside its original homeland usually indulges in nostalgia, no matter how it enjoys the present home. One of the most basic threads that connect these people to the original homeland is food. When the basic needs are satisfied, they will generally seek further gratification in things of less urgent need, such as items surrounding them at home. Following closely are the music and the performing arts of the homeland, these being part of the ambience in which they were brought up. Included also in these mental and emotional forms of gratification are reading materials. Most people want to know what happens in their homeland, so they read about them in the papers. There is a point beyond which the local media can no longer satisfy their needs, so papers and magazines are sent for from the homeland. While papers and magazines provide information of the present and the immediate past, another form of reading materials, literature, provides cultural links with the past, the present, and a peek into the likely future as well.

Over the years, there have been local Indonesian periodicals such as JAIA, AIA News, IKAWIRIA News, Suara PERWIRA, PWNI, Bulletin of ICEI, ICEI Newsletter and others. These provide, to varying degrees, some links with Indonesia, as well as a network among members of the community itself. Over the years also, the number of readers and subscribers of TEMPO, KOMPAS and other publications from Indonesia grew. Compared to the electronic media, the press gives people more detailed pictures of events and, what is more, what drives these events. While the community itself is the initiator, the reading of Indonesian press has now extended to those outside the community. This reflects the blurring of the border of the two countries in the course of the opening of the region. In fact, leading and high quality magazines and newspapers have been reaching out to the Australian community, not only bringing Indonesian versions of events that happen in Indonesia and overseas, but also revealing nuances in the language that mirror the Indonesian reader's psyche.

The language and the contents of the Indonesian press very much reflect the dynamism and the rapid development of the Indonesian civilisation, in the cultural as well as the intellectual sense. At the same time, the press in Indonesia also acts as the barometer of the society's attitudes, as well as the authorities' sense of security or insecurity vis-a-vis these attitudes. Take for example the popular woman's magazine FEMINA. The tenor of the magazine has developed from the concept of the woman as the nurturer and the husband's companion to the woman in the dual role of co-breadwinner and nurturer. Issues covered also have expanded to the law and the environment. The underlying theme of the battle for equality is becoming increasingly obvious, though measured. In the meantime, the men's magazine MATRA, now into its seventh year, deals with issues such as homosexuality, gigolos, extra-judicial marriages and other contentious issues, fairly openly.

Both Indonesian and Australian media exercise self-censorship, because what makes a particular publication or electronic medium better than their counterparts is, among others, their sense of social responsibility. Both Indonesian and Australian media, generally speaking, test the limits. The difference is, in Australia, what motivates the media to pull their heads in is the possible threats of litigation from individuals or organizations, while in Indonesia, as we have just witnessed recently, the media, apart from having to be careful to avoid litigation, also have the government and its whole configuration of ministers and hangers-on, to answer to, constantly.

In the fearless atmosphere of Australian media, the newspapers and magazines, and radio and television often, to varying degree of blatancy, depict a personality as an idiot, no matter how important a position he/she holds in the community. This is not possible in Indonesia. We still paint him/her as a personality of some importance, even if this person has proven to be a moron of late. This is probably because Indonesia is such a diverse society that people concede that a moron in the eyes of some might be regarded as a genius by others. In any issue, open confrontation is always avoided. What we did in TEMPO was to seek to cover as many aspects as possible of an issue, then it was up to the reader to highlight the parts that confirm their suspicions or allay their fears. This however, did not stop us from being accused of bias because we revealed a particular aspect at all, or, as recent events proved, condemned for reporting an issue of significant magnitude, because it put some people of power in a less than favourable light.

While I continuously seek my own place in Indonesian and Australian cultures, working as a journalist for *TEMPO* has helped me fine-tune this search.

Working in Indonesia for instance, I automatically assume the inherent, often involuntary, respect for the authorities. To interview a minister or a celebrity in Indonesia one needs to coax and cajole, while continuously admitting what a fantastic person, a high achiever, a blessing for humanity he/she is. Of course, in many cases, this is true. Australian ministers and celebrities are no less vulnerable to a high dose of flattery either, but mercifully, they are more used to being treated with less courtesy by the media here. In Indonesia, though conflicts in high places are regarded as relevant, because they may change the landscape of power in the government, they are covered in a less direct way. For instance, Bob Hawke's allegation that PM Keating once called Australia or described Australia as 'the arse end of the world' would not have been reported the way it was here. In fact, I suspect, a *TEMPO* editorial meeting would have decided not to report it at all.

Working in Australia I assume a greater degree of cynicism toward those who hold power, maybe because everything is more transparent, so one knows, more or less, how a person ascends to a position of power. In Indonesia, where transparency is not yet *de rigueur*, one gives the benefit of the doubt to those who manage to ascend to power, more so if they remain there.

The use of words in Indonesian media differs from that in Australian media. When an issue has political implications, Indonesian media tend to use euphemism. While in Australia an event where multiple shootings occur may be described as a massacre, regardless of who the perpetrators are, in Indonesia it may be described as an occurence, albeit an unfortunate one (*peristiwa*). It may also be described as multiple shootings, be they mysterious ones, or an armed conflict, if there is a skerrick of evidence that the other party tried to shoot back. Regardless of how this looks to readers in other countries, this is obviously the acceptable system in Indonesia.

Another form of reading material with no less importance in the community's life is literature. It is nostalgic, bonding, reinforcing, eye-opening and entertaining, regardless of whether the reader is very familiar or just faintly familiar with the background of a story, be it told in the form of a short story, a novel or a poem. Some, especially good ones, are also thought provoking. Literature, generally speaking, has a more lasting effect than the press, because the reader unconsciously enters the story, taking part in the journey, be it real or sentimental. While reading about an event in the press informs the reader, reading about an event or a series of events in a story influences the reader in a more profound way. A story, especially told in a novel, gives a cultural and temporal context, and affects the reader in a subliminal way. This is why, given the sense of responsibility demanded of the Indonesian media, a practitioner in Indonesian literature is expected to be particularly responsible and careful.

As a practitioner in this field, I find this responsibility put upon us somewhat restricting. For goodness sake, I have to be responsible as a journalist, can't I let loose my imagination in fiction?

Though there is no manual for a fiction writer, one knows that if one wants to be published in Indonesia, though the themes and content of the stories to be written are almost limitless, one has to be careful about certain things.

Generally, a quality story is expected to have a mission or a moral, to varying degrees of strength. If a person of high position, in secular or religious sense, is vilified in the story, then it has to be clear that he/she is separate from the rest of his/her community. For example, a religious leader is portrayed as corrupt: as the story unravels, the reader has to gain the understanding that he is a maverick of some kind, a black sheep in his religious community. It is also acceptable to elaborate on the temptations of an inherently saintly person, and his/her agony in overcoming them, provided this person does not slip off the rails in the end. Politicians are more vulnerable. Even so, only daring publications would publish stories that imply the corruptibility or the corrupt acts of politicians, especially if these are remotely recognisable. Pathos in the confusion resulting from transition from one authority to another, especially if the story does not explicitly apportion blame to the present authority, is acceptable.

Another sensitive issue is the morality of a woman, read: a good Indonesian woman. Despite the force of equality in the society, which has resulted among others, in increasing numbers of women having *relationships*, depicting these in stories is not acceptable. While a man who has been unfaithful to his wife can still be painted as a good man, provided he does not abandon his family, a woman who has been unfaithful to her husband is a fallen creature. An unfaithful husband can still be a good company director, minister of the state, minister of religion provided there is an explicit repentance, devoted father and so on, but an unfaithful wife is condemned for life. The closest that equality is portrayed, is in a story I read, where the female character nearly goes to bed with a man she obviously likes, but resorts to a cold shower instead because she doesn't want to be unfaithful to her fiance, from whom she is geographically separated. However, she is totally dismayed to hear later from her fiance that he, unlike her, has not been saving himself for her. The implied equality here is not in the act of disloyalty on the part of the woman, because she has not committed one, but in the admission that the woman has been extremely tempted, and in her anger expressed, not by throwing a tantrum, as usually expected and depicted of a woman, but by quietly questioning the values of the fiance.

So if I want to tell the story of a woman who has achieved a lot in life, is compassionate and a fairly good mother as well, I have to make sure there is no hanky-panky directly related to her. In the context of Australian literature, this kind of woman is a saint, which means she is dull and not easy to get along with. As a consequence, if I want to portray an achiever who is compassionate and a fairly good mother who occasionally slips off the rails, I have to make the character a non-Indonesian woman.

While an Australian novel will not sell if it does not have explicit sex in it, an Indonesian novel rarely has it. Sex, it appears, for Indonesians, is not an issue. Indonesians like it, and have plenty of it. But it is sufficient to allude, lightly or heavily, to it, leaving the reader to his/her own imagination. Besides, only *roman picisan*, trash, would depict explicit sex. The reason a quality novel can hardly depict explicit sex is because this is only sanctioned between married couples. Now who wants to read about a husband doing it with his wife, or a woman doing it with her husband? So what's the story in it? Is the husband impotent? Is the wife frigid? No? They both have healthy sexual drive? Then there's no issue. If one wants to read about explicit sex, read it in *roman picisan*, where a man does it with a woman of no virtue. So eroticism is a rarity in Indonesian literature. It is only acceptable in poetry. In any culture, a poet has more poetic licence than a prose writer.

While literature from the homeland is nostalgic, bonding, reinforcing, eye-opening and entertaining, we must not underestimate the importance of our own lives here. Many of us, and the second generation Indonesians, have life experiences specific to the blending of two cultures, two lifestyles and the multiple pressures and multiple fun resulting from them. The second generation especially, will have the benefit of the cultural heritage as well as the sense of freedom gained from being brought up in Australia. The potential for topics, content, themes and writing style is limitless. The literature coming out of this generation is no less important. In fact, you owe it to your children and their descendants to begin writing, if you are not already.

Chapter III
Looking Ahead:
Growth, Change and New directions

Cross-Cultural Marriages

Dr Ailsa & Mr Din Zainu'ddin

T: We have been asked to talk about *cross-cultural marriages*. We intend instead to talk about **a** cross-cultural marriage as our own is the only one we can presume to know. I don't intend to do all the talking and I can assure you that what either of us says arises from a great deal of animated discussion between us since Hilary's *perintah halus* [10] was applied. We hope our own experiences may have a broader relevance and resonance, specially for those of you who have also been involved in a cross-cultural marriage. As we have a script firmly in front of us to keep us within the time limit, I hope that you will excuse us if we read too fast and if we don't quite fit our forty years of experience into twenty minutes.

We'll begin by answering Janet Penny's opening question, 'How did you meet?' It was very mundane—no love at first sight; nothing like *Romeo and Juliet*. For one thing we were almost twice their age—I think she was about 13, wasn't she? We were both working in Canberra, both living in Havelock House and both allocated to the same table for meals. Din's first culture shock at Havelock was his first breakfast, when the sight of the word 'rice' led him to order 'rice bubbles' He ate them neat! Incidentally I imagine that you could hardly have a more valuable preparation for marriage than regular breakfast together. Then you are spared any shock in discovering what your partner is like first thing in the morning because you know already.

At that stage, we can both assure you, nothing was further from our thoughts than marriage. Shortly after we first met, Din even remarked in the course of conversation, that he could never marry a white woman as it could ruin his career as a diplomat. I found that reassuring. We could become friends without any complications. I had always intended to be a career woman and, back in the 1950s, marriage could certainly ruin a woman's plans for a career. I was already a research assistant and busy working on my M.A. thesis, which happened to be on '*The Bulletin* and Australian nationalism'. *The Bulletin's* racist slogan—'Australia for the **white** man'—and the articles and cartoons on that theme are quite incredible by today's standards. They were so appalling to me that I wanted to dissociate myself from that aspect of Australian nationalism and this looked like a good opportunity to enjoy friendship across racial barriers.

I was then a committed, ecumenical Methodist[11] and a member of the Student Christian Movement. I knew very little about Islam and was interested to discuss the differences and similarities between the two religions. There were more similarities than I had expected but, even so, for me to marry a Muslim was unthinkable. Obviously we both changed our minds in due course. For me the moment of truth came when Din said he was being posted to Moscow and I realised that I couldn't bear the thought of never seeing him again.

---

10 Gentle pressure (used ironically!)

11 I have it on good authority that I am now a secular Methodist.

Z: For me it was when I was convinced that Tommy was about to become engaged to an Australian friend she had known for some years.

T.: We then quickly discovered that anyone contemplating a cross-cultural marriage is inevitably given a great deal of well-meaning but often ill-informed advice. Even the most ecumenical of my Student Christian Movement friends found it hard to come to terms with marriage to a Muslim—'but he can have four wives!' they said—which was about all that most Australians knew about Islam in those days. Several friends were also concerned about the children of a mixed marriage. One assured me that 'they will curse you for bringing them into the world'. Even well-informed advice can be counterproductive when offered to two moderately stubborn people and ultimately, as with any marriage, when nothing that could be said against it seemed to us to matter any more, that seemed to be a good case for it. We needed to be a little more sure to make up for our friends and acquaintances on both sides being a lot less sure.

Z.: Then the problems began in earnest. When I told a colleague in Jakarta about our plans his response was 'Don't!' His arguments, mainly to do with *career prospects*, no longer mattered to me because by then I knew that I really wanted to study economics and then work in a rural development bank.

Then there was the *religious difference*. I am a Moslem and Tommy a Christian. I was liberal enough not to raise the matter of conversion at all. I only insisted on a Moslem wedding and that the children should be Moslem.

T.: I knew that conversion was quite impossible for either of us and, as I took religious commitment very seriously, I could not have contemplated nominal conversion. I assumed that we would be living in Indonesia where the children would naturally be brought up as Moslem but I also believed that, in the last resort, the decision would rest with them - as it has.

We also assumed, without any need for discussion that we would each retain our own *nationality*, something which would have been impossible for me prior to the 1936 Nationality Act.[12] Later on, once Din was eligible for Australian naturalisation, there would be a yearly phone call from Immigration to tell us so. 'Yes,' I would say, 'we know that.' 'It would be administratively easier if he were to be naturalised', the voice would say—a different one each year. We knew *that* only too well from experience at various airports which classified us differently but I would say sweetly, 'Yes but *your* administrative convenience does not seem to be adequate reason for *him* to change his nationality.' I might have added that he wouldn't lightly throw away something which he had fought to obtain.

Z.: We faced the worst case scenario when it looked as if the West Irian issue could lead to open warfare. It seemed very likely at the time. Would we go or stay? I said I'd face

12 For a worst case scenario which did happen see 'Rose Inagaki: 'Is it a crime to marry a foreigner?' in M. Lake and F. Kelly, *Double Time. Women in Victoria - 150 years*, Penguin Australia, 1985 pp. 335-43

internment here as it would be less disruptive for the girls and Tommy had a job here. *Now* we know better than to take press demands for strong action so seriously.

Tommy was an Australian planning to marry an Indonesian but she didn't know anything about the *life in Indonesia*. I insisted that she should go there first with no strings attached. There was a newly established intergovernmental scheme for which Tommy was eligible so she went to Indonesia as a Volunteer Graduate.

T.: I had been at the historic National Conference of the Australian Student Christian Movement in Canberra where Don Anderson spoke about the scheme in front of the leaders of both sides of Parliament. There may have been no strings attached but my own mind was pretty firmly made up, as I told the Volunteer Graduates, who then had to decide whether this was acceptable PEGAWAI [13] behaviour or a danger to the scheme.

I then went off to Indonesia believing that I was going for good—otherwise I'd have left a few of my nine cases of books behind. When I met Din's colleague, I was told that I should refuse Din for his own good. Hoping I was being suitably *halus*, [14] I said that I really felt Din should make his own decision on the matter and that, if he should wish to change his mind, I would accept that.

Z.: *The actual marriage* was complicated to arrange. The *penghulu* argued that Tommy should be converted. I was Moslem and my wife's religion was one of those based on a holy book so she didn't need to be Moslem. I said, 'I know that rule' and they had to agree. Next I went to the civil registry to get the marriage certificate and was told that an Indonesian couldn't marry a white woman.
I asked, 'What regulation is that?'
He said, 'It's from the Dutch law.'
Z.: 'If I am not mistaken we are now an independent nation!'
Official.: 'But Dutch law still applies.'
Z.: 'Well, I've seen Indonesian men married to Dutch women in the past.'
O.: 'They were *high ranking* men.'
Z.: 'So what do you mean by 'high-ranking'?'
O.: 'They were senior civil servants.'
Z.: 'What about the army?'
O.: 'An army man must be an officer.'
Z.: 'I am an officer of the Indonesian Republican Army so give us our marriage certificate.'
So he did.

T.: I didn't feel properly married without the Methodist marriage service so we read that together on the morning of our marriage[15], with Herb acting as possibly the world's first marriage celebrant—a truly ecumenical meeting of believers, one for each of the three holy books—except that he didn't actually proclaim us man and wife. We then went off for the

---

13 Member of the **P**lan for the **E**mployment of **G**raduate **A**ustralians to **W**ork **A**s **I**ndonesians.

14 Refined.

15 I omitted any promise to 'obey', but promised to love and honour. My first insubordination?

Muslim part of the wedding at the Gambir Office of the Penghulu—nerve-racking on a Friday morning as I was afraid the office would close before we were through. Fortunately it didn't.

Z.: Once I had left the foreign service and the army I faced the *problem of re-employment*. To begin my work in rural banking I needed to study economics. I applied to become an economics student at the University of Indonesia but was refused because I did not have a Senior High School certificate. I would have had to start by studying for that first. Then a friend sent Tommy an advertisement for a teacher of Indonesian at Melbourne University and I applied, though with little hope of success. Norman Harper, Chair of the Board of Indonesian Studies, came to Jakarta to interview candidates. I said I would go to Melbourne if I could study at the university as well. The interview was at the time of the General Election of 1955 and I took him to see various polling booths. Jakarta's streets were deserted that day, apart from a few army jeeps, so our car was the only one in sight at the time. Perhaps that impressed him!

T.: A magnificent Morris Minor!

Z.: Of course, when I did get the job, there were *teaching problems*. We came to Melbourne in March 1956 with our three-week-old daughter, who had to be exempted from the Immigration Restriction Act. I had taught Indonesian at Ford Foundation for half a year, mostly conversation. John Echols, from Cornell, was in Jakarta when I was accepted and I asked his advice. He showed me material based on the Direct Method. In addition I had Sutan Muhammad Zain's Indonesian grammar, another by Dr Fokker—and there was Pino. I had to devise a full Indonesian course from them, and my English wasn't the best. I don't know how I came to accept that position—the boldness of youth and the desire to have an opportunity to study at University, I suppose.

Some big *money problems* came with the job. I was a fixed term Lecturer, employed for six years. The salary was not even enough for day to day living, let alone for University fees. Tommy's parents provided accommodation for a year. Then we rented a one-bedroom flat. I asked Professor Harper for permission to teach outside as well. I taught two nights a week at CAE and worked at weekends for Radio Australia, translating news bulletins.

By the time Lisa was born, Tommy had casual jobs—correcting matriculation exams, writing scripts for the Women's Section of Radio Australia which I translated, doing the preliminary research for Australian Dictionary of Biography articles, typing for Nettie Palmer. In 1959 my mother came for a year's visit. We had moved to another one-bedroom flat with a passage wide enough to provide sleeping quarters for the children. Mak slept in the one other all-purpose room. She rejoined us after a year back in Indonesia and so our family then became an extended one and we moved into larger rented quarters.

I had *study problems* too. As a full time lecturer I had to learn entirely by myself how to teach Indonesian. I had no language teaching colleagues in the Indonesian Studies Department and absolutely no collegiality from anyone in the wider university. I had to study English grammar more thoroughly to understand how it differed from Indonesian and to prepare the material to be roneoed for students. My best reference for English grammar was my mother-in-law. We really enjoyed discussing points of grammar with each other. I don't know why people dislike their mothers-in-law. I loved my mother-in-law.

As I wanted to return to Indonesia as soon as we could, I undertook more study than I could possibly manage, with not very pleasing results. I had to grapple with those studies in English as well and I often nodded off in lectures, specially after lunch at siesta time. I could not manage to take many lecture notes, so I just read the required books. Before the six years of my contract ended I left—much to the surprise of Jamie Mackie. He was in charge of Indonesian Studies by then. He said, 'How can you live without this income?' I still remember telling him, 'Don't worry, Jamie! I am a Minangkabau!' He even contacted Tommy and asked 'Is he serious?'

T.: I said, 'Of course he is. We have discussed it, you know.' I had managed to obtain regular employment in the Law School at Melbourne University, tutoring in British History (Law)—mainly constitutional history and not my preferred area—on a tutor's salary, not my preferred level! It was even less than Din's inadequate lecturer's salary. It required careful budgeting. As an insurance policy for the future, I enrolled in a part-time Dip. Ed. course. As I enjoyed it, I decided to complete B.Ed. That was to prove a useful decision.

Z.: Little did I realise that for me there was still almost the same amount of work. I started the course in Indonesian part-time at Tintern Girls Grammar School, again having to create class materials for various levels. I continued teaching at the Council of Adult Education and doing casual work at Radio Australia on the least popular shifts. The only advantage of part-time work was that I could adjust my working hours to look after the children when Tommy was working. Both of us were also active in the various Australian Indonesian groups being established.

By the early '60s I was beginning to realise that it was too late to achieve my ambition of working in rural banking - I was already 39 and, in addition, the children had started at school in Australia. We had to consider the problem of their education and general upbringing. One parent must work full time and the other part time so I said to Tommy, 'Choose which one. You or me?' She chose the full time option and started to apply for appropriate full time work. As it looked as if we must plan for a future in Australia, I did my Dip. Ed. as I was likely to continue teaching Indonesian part-time—indeed I haven't quite stopped up till now.

T.: I did not believe that we could make a final decision about staying in Australia until Din had visited Indonesia again. We all went in the summer vacation 1966-7, hindered by a Qantas strike and financed in part by a travel grant from Monash Education Faculty, where I had already found a tenured position. I should say that, while some eyebrows rose at the idea of my full time work, a great many more rose a lot higher at the idea of a husband who did **not** have full time employment. I believe this was one instance of our ability to make our own choices simply because we were on the margins of two societies and so could choose with impunity what suited us from either one.

This has happened in a number of other ways too. Some years after my father died, we moved in with my mother, quite a Minangkabau thing to do. It meant that we each had a mother and mother-in-law living together, a three generation extended family which has astounded a great many Australian friends. On the matter of language my mother had already begun learning Indonesian and Din's mother soon picked up enough English for bilingual conversations to take place. On the matter of food there was no problem for me as long as I provided meals which included rice and *sambal*, although the latter was not very easy to find thirty years ago. When my mother-in-law arrived she explained to me firmly that, according to *adat*, an older woman did not cook when there was a younger woman in the house but she did give me an occasional demonstration lesson which I attempted to codify—and finished up with a cookbook.[16] If you read its introduction you'll see how quintessentially mid-60s it is.

We are still working on the question of **cultural rules and value themes** which are rather more complex than the media would lead us to believe or than we can tackle in brief. Jenny Noesjirwan's opening address at the 1985 Winter Lecture Series, *Nearest Southern Neighbour*, deals very well with that question.[17]

Conclusion

Tonight's session is actually entitled *Looking Ahead* Let me do that briefly before concluding.

Nationally speaking, Australians have almost adopted an inversion of the Indonesian national motto: *Bhinneka tunggal ika* ['Unity in diversity' or 'Many becoming one']. This is exemplified in the song 'We are one but we are many' and, as in Indonesia, intermarriage will speed that process. Cross-cultural and multicultural activities in general have taken a giant step forward in the past forty years although, on present trends and indications, the institution of marriage itself may have a more problematic future.

As for the sub-title, *Growth, change and new directions*, we believe that these are three elements essential for the survival of any partnership, especially marriage—*any* marriage. The more initial differences there are, the more growth and change will be required of both partners and the more new directions they are likely to explore. The more prepared partners are for the possibility of differences, the more likely it is that they can work out a viable compromise.

This change is occurring in a changing society. Although it was not acknowledged by White Anglo-Saxon Protestant Australians in the 1950s, Australia was already multicultural—as, indeed, it has always been at least since 1788—and was in the process of becoming very much more diverse. Our children seem quite happy to have been brought into the world but that aspect of intermarriage we'll leave to Karen.

16 *How to Cook Indonesian Food*, AIA of Victoria, 1965, Revised edn 1967, 1971

17 Based on her doctoral research, 'Cross-cultural contact between Indonesians and Australians', it was a topic of more than academic interest to her and her Minangkabau husband as well as to me and mine. ''There is something I don't know....': a discussion of the cross-cultural experience' in *Nearest Southern Neighbour: Some Indonesian views of Australia and Australians*, Monash University, 1986, pp. 19-29] The final panel discussion, 'Servantless Superwomen?' included cross-cultural comparisons of marriage.

As for our specific topic, 'Cross-cultural marriages', if we return to *Romeo and Juliet* again for a minute, we might reflect that their problems arose from a family feud with no cross-cultural elements at all. I myself would also argue that every marriage has to cross the widest cultural divide of all—the one between masculine and feminine cultures.

In concluding I would like to quote an article entitled 'The Marriage of True Minds', which appeared in *Djembatan: Quarterly Newsletter of the Volunteer Graduate Association for Indonesia* in 1959 [18] without attribution. As editor of that newsletter I can assure you that the author wrote from her own limited experience and that her marriage did endure. She posed the question: 'Is inter-racial marriage to be encouraged, condoned or condemned?'

After arguing that 'it is as impossible to answer this question in general terms as it would be to answer a similar question about marriage itself,' she concluded that 'It all depends on the two individuals concerned. It is probably even more true than of marriage in general that it should not be entered upon lightly, wantonly or ill-advisedly. With this qualification my own answer would be:

> 'Let me not to the marriage of true minds
> Admit impediments.'

Those are indeed my own sentiments.

I also believe that the organiser of this year's Winter Lecture Series has shown great courage in experimenting with this new format. It will provide an interesting challenge to prepare for publication. Tackling contemporary history can be full of pitfalls and no two people, even in the one marriage, will necessarily remember the past in the same way. We've been burrowing around among past letters, bulletins, diaries and old copies of *Djembatan, AIA News* and *JAIA* as a direct effect of these lectures. I'm sure Hilary hopes that others have been doing the same and that lots of documentary material will appear for use in next year's *JAIA*.

Note: T represents Tommy, Ailsa's nickname.

---

18 Vol. III, Nos 1 & 2, pp. 13-16

Second and Third Generations: Pleasant Aromas of Cheese and Durian

Dr Karen Sri Kartomi Thomas

Ibu-ibu, Bapak-Bapak yang saya hormati:

I am the product of a mixed marriage. My Javanese father came to Australia in the 1950s on the Colombo Plan and my mother lived and studied in Adelaide at the time. Being the child of these two people has placed me in the position of the recipient of the best of both worlds: my mother tongue is English and my chosen profession is the field of Indonesian.

When I first put on my thinking cap to ponder throughtfully about the question of, 'Who are the second-generation Indonesians in Victoria?' I found myself in a quandry. Am I classified as a second-generation Indonesian if I am not a full-blooded Indonesian? If my family had lived in Indonesia would I then become second-generation Australian? Moreover does being a child of a mixed marriage qualify me to speak on behalf of other mixed children?

I considered the lives of Indonesian and mixed Indonesian and Australian friends of my age and concluded that each one of us has pursued such different directions. We need only take a cursory look at the profiles published in the *Ikawiria* Newsletter periodically over the last few months about various second-generation Indonesians, both full-blooded and mixed, to grasp how differently each one of us has turned out and how each one of us has made choices unique to our individual aspirations.

I concluded then, that I qualify to speak simply about myself as a example of second-generation Indonesian-Australian. Perhaps those of you who have descended from one or two Indonesian migrants have lived in Australia for a large part of your life, might see some similarities between your experiences and mine.

My affiliation with the Indonesian community in Victoria to date has played a special role in the course of my life. In the 1970s I vividly remember weekly Indonesian dancing lessons dominating my teenage years. My school friends spent their weekends doing Australian pastimes, such as playing netball or going to the movies. 'What are you doing this Satuday afternoon, Karen?' they often asked me. As if my plans were the most Australian thing to do, I replied with an air of confidence, 'I'm going to my Indonesian dancing lessons', and suddenly a glazed look would seep accross their faces; they had no conception of what Indonesian dancing lessons entailed.

I studied Javanese dance and later Balinese and Sumatran dance from various professional Indonesian dancers living in Melbourne or visiting Melbourne. In later years I spent some time in Yogyakarta learning *Serimpi* and also in Jakarta sudying the Sundanese *Tari Topeng Kelana*. I enjoyed all kinds of dance: I began with ballet and played Alice in a ballet production of Alice in Wonderland at the age of ten and in my twenties I turned my hand (or should I say my feet) to ballroom dancing. Every year I performed the Indonesian dances I had learnt at important events such as *Hari Kemerdekaan* (Independence Day), *Lebaran*, other community functions, at schools, at festivals such as those held at the National Gallery in the Great Hall and at Indonesian concerts made possible by the Monash Music Department held at Monash Alexander Theatre and the Robert Blackwood Hall. I remember, for example, playing the *kijang emas* (the golden deer) in the *Ramayana* dance drama. I enjoyed wearing the brightly coloured costumes and sensing the nervous vibes of my fellow dancers also around my age. Above all, I experienced a gradual awareness of a crucial component of any performance: the presence of an audience. initially I simply danced on stage what I had learnt during my lessons. Soon, however, after someone had expressed to me a friendly, 'Why don't you smile?' I discovered that smiling for the audience infinitely improved my performance.

While learning Indonesian dance informally, I studied Indonesian language formally at Presbyterian Ladies' College. I received first prize for an Indonesian essay in my final year awarded by VILTA (Victorian Indonesian Language Teaching Association). In the 1980s I majored in Indonesian at Monash University and was very fortunate to become an exchange student at the University of California Berkeley. A few years later I obtained a Masters of Arts at Berkley and I then embarked on a PhD. My supervisor at the time tactfully stated to me, 'Be sure to *like* your topic because not only will you breath it but you will live it for the next x number of years.' It did indeed permeate every aspect of my life. I had an exciting project—modern Indonesian theatre—which presented me with the opportunity in 1989 and 1990 to meet such well known directors as Rendra, Riantiarno and Dindon about whom I eventually wrote. I met other well known directors such as Ikranegara, Teguh Karya, Putu Wijaya and Ratna Sarumpaet all of whom gracoiusly gave me little of their time. Like most doctoral dissertation the project became a gruelling exercise to finish. What I had done in the community as a performer for the last twenty years however, gave me some of the energy to perservere with the project to the end.

When I returned to Melbourne and began teaching Indonesian part-time at Victoria College (now known as Deakin University) and the AIA, and later full-time at Melbourne University, my teaching techniques to some extent evolved to become performance oriented. Role-plays, particularly in the beginning stages of language learning and full length plays by the time the students have reached advanced levels, have in my experience enabled them to progress remarkably well. My involvement in the Indonesian community has played not only a major role in my choice of profession, but my teaching approach has been directly influenced by opportunities which began with those Saturday afternoon Indonesian dancing lessons.

My interest in performance however, was truly nurtured in my home. My father often performed on stage in the 1970s singing folk songs and *kroncong*. He took part in a Sundanese *calung* ensemble which performed humorous skits punctuated and accompanied by the *calung*. My mother, now Head of the Music Department at Monash University, one of the many caps she wears, is an accomplished pianist; over the years she has often accompanied my father singing, my grandfather on the violin and many other musicians and choirs and guided me in my own piano practice. As I grew up she frequently ferried me to orchestral, ballet amd opera performances; and each Christmas we sang Christmas carols around the piano.

Apart from the specific opportunities of performance, the community has provided me with a broader source of unflagging assistance. It plays the role of an emotional support shifting back and forth in my imagination. Since having a baby nearly eight months ago I have had considerably less time to participate in community events and even more so since recently returning to full time work. The community continues to hover in my mind. I feel its presence through such newsletters as those published by *Ikawiria* and AIA, through the community radio, through lecture series and through knowledge of community events spread by word of mouth. Its existence presents an extremely potent resource.

Furthermore, the community has played the role of informant. As a child of an Indonesian migrant I was inevitably taken to Indonesia. On each of our visits I had no choice but to communicate in Indonesian, to participate in the culture and to adhere to accepted behavioural norms. I began leaps and bounds ahead of my Australian counterparts who did not have the opportunity to be informed by a larger Indonesian community. Nor did my Australian counterparts grow up under the influence of an Indonesian man married to an Australian woman who herself took a great interest in Indonesia. Our home frequently became the venue for Indonesian sing-alongs. We had them so often that on one occasion I pondered quietly to myself, 'Don't they know any other songs?' I had to admit that deep down I enjoyed hearing the same Christmas carols year after year around the piano. I used to watch my father eat rice twice daily and simultaneously hear him exclaim that no Indonesian feels that he has eaten properly until he has had a plate of rice. In turn he used to watch me enjoying chunks of cheese with a puzzled look on his face. 'Doesn't that cheese smell bad to you?' he would ask. I know durian has a reputation for its delicious and delicate flavour. Unfortunately, however, I have never been able to embrace its rather overwhelming aroma joyously.

Many more examples of my homelife abound, illustrating that I have had ample opportunity to attune myself to Indonesian culture. In particular, after each visit to Indonesia, I became acutely aware of the meaning of polite behaviour which differed markedly from its meaning in Australia. I learned, for example, that a burp after a meal shows your appreciation for the food. I learned from my grandmother, who chewed betel and lives in Kroya in the Banyumas area of Central Java, that you need not think twice about speaking with your mouth full, or that you may proudly turn your head to spit out the juice of the betel into a spitoon. I learned in later years that if you wish to purchase stamps at the post office you simply push and shove your way to the front of the counter; you do not wait politely to be served. Examples of such behaviour in an Australian post office could incur the wrath of certain Australian customers. If you push and shove in an Indonesian post office, however, doing so does not indicate inpoliteness; that is simply the way it is.

Many might interpret my views on burping and chewing and pushing and shoving as tolerance on my part. However I perceive them not as tolerance but as ready acceptance of the simple reality that more than one way of being polite exists and that the shape of such an important behavioural norm is culture bound.

The community has always been and always will be a remarkable, dynamic, supportive and informative structure and a helpful stepping stone to Indonesia. Even before venturing to

Indonesia, the community broadens the horizons and opportunities of us all in Australia. Those Indonesians and Australians who have associated consistently with the malleable community body over the years, stand as the pillars of the structure, while the many new faces offer ideas and renewed enthusiasm.

What then does the future hold for second generation Indonesian-Australians? In my view, the community will continue to provide a supportive base to its members. I dearly hope that my daughter, now a member of the third generation, benefits from the community on an emotional and informative level as I have. In her baby-ish fashion she has in the last week discovered how to twist her wrist. This action could conceivably become the basis of hand movements of an Indonesian dancer. Indeed, her newly acquired flexibility in the wrist and her ability to laugh, together are perfect prerequisites to becoming the next badminton champion. (I do have high aspirations of her; ultimately, however, the pathway she takes will be of her own choosing).

Despite increasing economic interest in Indonesia many Australian business people approaching Indonesia continue to do so in blissful ignorance. As the community grows larger with the third generation well on its way, the more understanding of Indonesia Australia becomes. The current political drive to improve relations between Indonesia and Australia and the obstacles such a drive faces, will dissipate as the community spreads its tentacles further; for if, on an emotional level, Australians felt supported rather than threatened by neighbouring Indonesia, mutual understanding and therefore relations would in my view, improve no end.

Since more and more Australian secondary schools offer Indonesian, I envisage more and more Australians joining the community. This contrasts markedly with my school days where learning Indonesian placed you in the minority group. The prospect that next year many Victorian primary schools will offer Indonesian at year 6 is an exciting one. Furthermore, the other day my husband, looking through the Camberwell local newspaper, discovered a Kindergarten in Mont Albert which teaches Indonesian. The third generation, along-side with other Australians, I hope will remain very much attuned with Indonesia. I hope they know even more than my generation about Indonesian language and culture. In our home my father often quoted the saying, 'knowledge is power'. With knowledge we have the power to overcome obstacles: with knowledge, cultural differences can suddenly cease to be a threat because they no longer take such a foreign shape.

Educational Directions

Zulfikar Alimuddin

Introduction

First of all, I would like to say that this is a truly great honour and privilege for me to stand here before all of you to share my views about educational directions as an Indonesian student studying here in Australia. In pursuing this discussion I am going to try to be as general as possible, yet in many instances I will refer to my personal experience and perceptions as illustration or examples; in doing so I try to portray the common knowledge underlying such examples or perceptions. By the end of this session I would like people to think that my talk is not a mere personal opinion, because it is based on knowledge obtained in generality. I know this is not an easy task for me, especially given my limited experience and knowledge, but I will do my best.

Discussion

To start with, probably the most important question that we should ask is, why it is important to discuss this issue at all ? I think there could be many reasons to discuss this issue. Firstly, statistics have shown that the number of Indonesian students coming to Australia keeps increasing. Significant increase has occurred since the year of 1986 (please refer to the graphs in the next pages) This means Australian 'education' will have more and more impact on Indonesian people.

Secondly, I strongly believe that we share a common understanding that education is a subset of our society's complexities. Education influences people in dealing with problems, while at the same time problems educate people. Education thus determines how people interpret and value their experience (McCall, 1978). In the light of the Australian and Indonesian relationships, the education that Indonesian students have here will then influence them in interpreting any phenomena which might affect the two countries in the future. Also, since the future emerges from the present which itself developed from the past, then we should really understand the past, and particularly the present, in an endeavour to anticipate changes in the structure and function of society in the future.

Before we proceed, at this stage we might need to agree on the framework of thinking about what we mean by education. We should make it really clear whether we are discussing educational direction in its broad sense, as an activity that goes on spasmodically in almost any human intercourse, or education in the sense of that which is carried out in the education system (Chanan and Gilchrist, 1974).

I am going to pursue my discussion in the light of the first perspective where the second perspective should come as a subset of the first one, also education which is pursued or experienced by students **not** in their home country.

Now, to give us a better illustration of what education has really brought about in many aspects of our life, in terms of the relations among countries, I would like to show you some of the facts relating to this matter.

In the light of our purposes, what has education actually achieved in terms of relations between Australia and Indonesia? Honestly, I have not been able to gather direct references on a large scale, however I did manage to get some of the perspectives on the benefits gained from international students in the past, both for Australia and the countries from where those international students came. And since Indonesian students formed a large proportion of international students, I assumed that these perspectives apply to the Australia-Indonesia relationship to some extent.

The Sydney Committee for Overseas Students said that :

> *Government to government contacts are made easier and there is a greater understanding and tolerance of cultural differences (submission No.9, p.2) (Industry Commission, 1991)*

The South Australian Government said :

> *While it is not possible to assess these (cultural and educational) benefits in dollars, the networks formed are significant. Many students return to their home countries to become senior government and business leaders. (Several Ministers in Asian countries are graduates of the University of Adelaide for example.) Such a network enables high level contacts to be pursued by South Australian institutions and government officials (Submission No.79, p.2) (Industry Commission, 1991)*

The South Australian Government also said :

> *At all levels, there is the opportunity to share both educationally and culturally expanding horizons and levels of tolerance and understanding. Friendships and connections can flow on from this into potential and business networks of the future ....(Submission No.79, p.7) (Industry Commission, 1991)*

Professor Wells from the Graduate School of Management and Public Policy, Sydney University said :

> *Young business managers who receive their training in a foreign country are drawn to that country when trading opportunities arise later in their careers. Business follows where education has led!!! This is a very powerful draw for international trade (Submission No.3, p.7). (Industry Commission, 1991)*

How can we perceive these facts from the view of social processes as part of education ?
Blan postulates that :

> *When people are thrown together, and before common goals or role expectations have crystallized among them, the advantages to be gained from entering into exchange relations furnish incentives for social interaction, thus fostering the development of a network of social relations and a rudimentary group structure. (the Open University, 1972)*

I hope these facts can serve as long-range results of international education. To achieve those results we might need to look at the education process while a student is here in Australia. Yet, education is not a new setting, instead it is developed on values which have been built previously. What I am saying is that when a student comes here to study, with him/her he/she also brings values and understandings. The challenge is how they are going to survive with those values or understanding and how much would 'Australian culture' have influenced them, if not changed them, as persons. What kind of persons will they be when they leave this country for their home ?

From this point, I will refer to my own experience and perception about the education that I am explaining here. Like other people, I suppose, when I came here, I came with certain expectations and also my social expectation (Indonesian society) which had been built in me. I might at that time have had my own prejudices about Australia and its people. I had developed these preconceptions and prejudices from what I heard or saw on television or movies, or what I read in magazines or newsletters. Is this a common phenomenon? According to McCall (1978), people perceive and interpret other people and objects in terms of their meanings to them. It follows that their definitions and classifications only in part reflect the 'real nature' of things. People create, as much as they define, the meanings of things, and as we have seen, there is a large class of social objects that 'exist' only as created and collectively understood meanings.

Some of the prejudices that I held which I would like to share with you are :

1. I used to believe that Australian people were not kind and friendly. This was quickly eliminated by some experiences I had on my second day after arrival when a lady offered her help to find my, I should really say our, apartment. She drove us to the address that we had. On the following day, someone returned my friend's wallet which was lost that morning. In that wallet, there was some money as well as credit cards and some identification. These experiences did not only change my perception (so fast?) but also created a new image about how honest Australian people were.

(By meeting more and more people and getting more experiences, the image of friendly people was strengthening, while the image of very honest people did not stay as strong as it was.)

2. I used to tend to think that Australia was a very efficient and productive country until I then had my industrial experience in some industries.

Next, how has my education here influenced or partly shaped me as a person ? My formal education and involvement in social activities have allowed me to gain broader perspectives about Australia in quite a wide range of aspects. My formal education has given me the opportunity to explore more about the education system in Australia. My campus provides me (and other students as well, of course) with the opportunities to engage in learning activities. My interaction with my classmates introduced me to new perspectives and appreciation about life, world, religion, marriage, and so on and so forth.

However, it is my socialization, I think, which has really allowed me to explore more about this country and its social values. I would like to share with you some of my invaluable experience gained through my 'education process.'

a. My involvement with the Indonesian Students Association started when I and some friends revived the association which had not been active for quite some time. It was more like establishing a new organization. In the process of building this, I could get to learn how to deal with the authorities in my Institution (RMIT). Given the nature of my position in the organization for two years, I also got to meet people, Australian and Indonesian, and then shared our views. In fact, this was when I met Mrs. Da Costa for the first time, and now she has invited me to speak tonight because of my involvement in the organization. I also learned how people here appreciated our nation so much (probably as much as they critisize our political systems) through some activities that we hosted, like an Indonesian culture night for two consecutive years, 1992 at RMIT and 1993 at the Melbourne Town Hall. Hosting this kind of event, in fact, not only allowed me (and friends) to exercise our skills in many aspects, but also opened a bigger window for us to identify how people responded to our culture. Furthermore, people's response has actually made me realize that I have quite a rich culture.

b. I also participated in the international student activities at our campus. My position in 1993 as the association's liaison for RMIT Union gave me the first insight into how Australians hold their formal meetings. To be honest, I was totally lost in the first meeting. My involvement in the same association this year, in a position with greater and wider responsibilities, forced me not only to know the issues and problems faced by international students, but also to analyse and constructively critisize the Australian education system (at RMIT particularly).

c. Probably, one of the most challenging experiences I had is how to cope with social expectations in this society, which in many instances are different from what have been developed in me. Things like calling people by their names is not easy for me, honestly; while at the same time I know that it would be O.K for me to call Mrs. Da Costa by her first name, Hilary, I find it hard to do so. So I call her Mrs. Hilary instead. A compromise, but not correct. I could go on and on about this but I think the message will not be much different.

With all of these things in mind, how do I envisage myself in the near future when I finish my study and go back to Indonesia? I hope, with all of these experiences, knowledge and perceptions I will have further developed during my education here; I will be able to be a person with a wiser and broader view, a person who can see phenomena from many different angles, and thus be able to understand other people better. So it is not merely connections and networks which I am going to expect, which are superficial to me, but a deep understanding, so that I can make compromises between my perceptions and other people's perceptions.

I think this should be our ultimate aim in having international education between Australia and Indonesia.To conclude this presentation I would like to thank 'learning' for the richness that it has given to me, to you, to all of us.

References :

Chanan G. and Gilchrist L., *What Education is For*, Methuen & CO. Ltd., London, 1974.

Industry Commission - Report No.12 August 14, 1991, *Exports of Education Services*, Australian Government Publishing Service, Canberra, 1991.

McCall G.J. and Simmons J.L., *Identities and Interaction*, The Free Press-a Division of Macmillan Publishing Co., Inc., New York, 1978.

The Open University, *Social Interaction - The Sociological Perspective Units 5-8*, Eyre & Spottiwoode Ltd., Great Britain, 1972.

Table 1: Student Arrivals from Selected Asian Countries

	1983/84	1984/85	1985/86	1986/87	1987/88	1988/89	1989/90	1990/91
China (a)	214	482	728	2038	7878	13224	24269	4774
Hong Kong	1139	1529	1420	1871	4024	5186	8483	8105
Indonesia	1743	2214	2390	3181	4117	4666	5589	6043
Japan	607	998	1076	1607	2675	4285	4481	4657
Korea	172	199	353	762	2051	2295	2848	3274
Malaysia	7268	8022	8139	8193	8226	8604	9028	8054
Singapore	1178	1316	1258	1541	2465	3055	4449	4447
Thailand	520	689	730	1206	2603	3688	2440	2345
Other	1060	1447	1644	1750	2260	2806	4860	3582
TOTAL	**13901**	**16896**	**17738**	**22149**	**36299**	**47809**	**66447**	**45281**

(a) Includes Taiwan

Growth of Student Arrivals from Selected Asian Countries

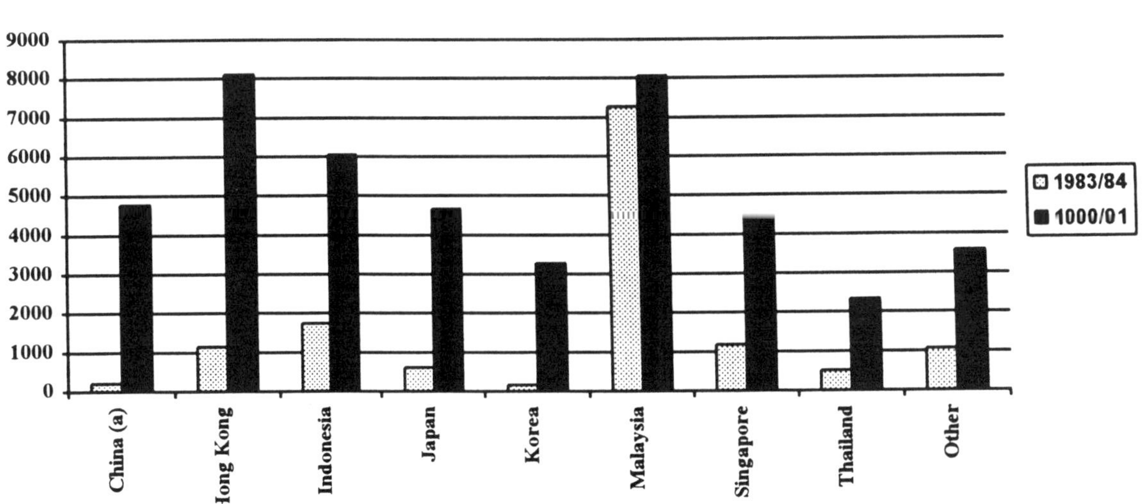

Student Arrivals by Region of Last Residence

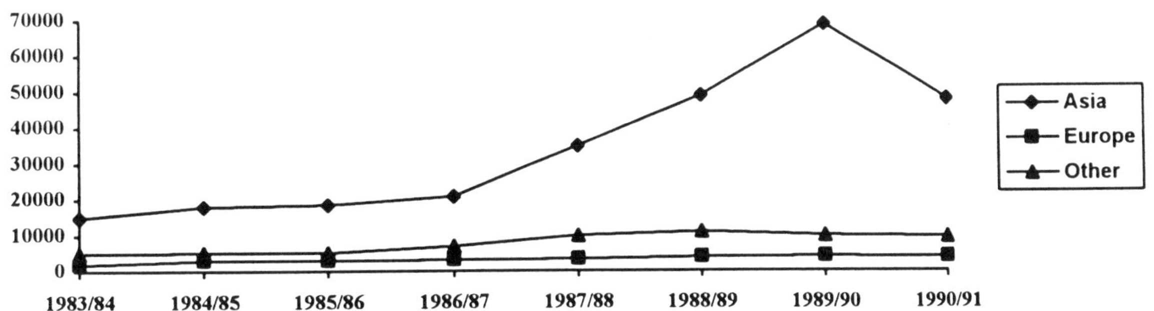

Overseas Students in Australia as at 30 June 1986 to 1990

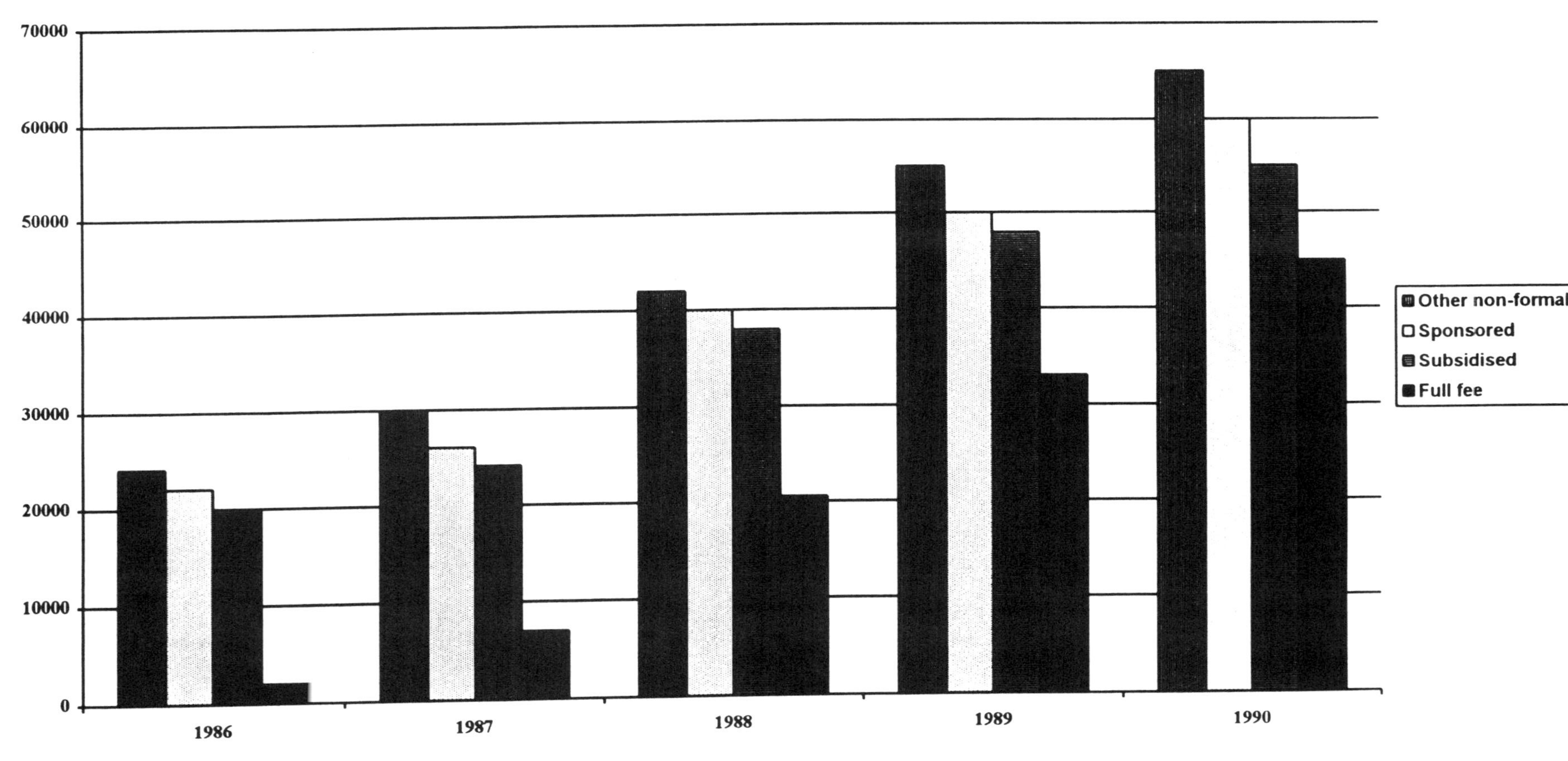

Note: Other non-formal includes categories such as exchange students, occupational and religious trainees and military personeel.
Source: DEET

Growth, Change and New Directions in Education

Lanita Idrus

The topic of growth, change and new directions in education as it relates to both the Indonesian community in Victoria and also to the Australia-Indonesia relationship is a huge subject for discussion. Indeed my paper this evening will not be able to cover every aspect of the topic.

In fact, I wish to limit my discussion by focusing on 2 things: 1) the experience of Indonesians in the processes of education in Victoria; and 2) the outcomes of education, followed by my personal observations of the trends and possible new directions in education for Indonesian residents, transitory Indonesians in Victoria primarily, and Australia generally, and concluding with a view of what education means for Australia's bilateral relations with Indonesia.

Education in Context

Firstly, I'd like to begin by offering a definition of education in order to place our dialoge in context.

Contrary to popular belief, education is not just schooling. The term schooling suggests compulsory and conscious efforts at attaining a standard of cognitive and psychomotor achievement necessary for a particular goal such as completion of VCE or HSC or Matriculation (as it was referred to in the 'good old days').

Rather, education is much more than schooling, it is lifelong endeavour. It refers to the sum of all that one learns both consciously and subliminally, or formally and informally, which is then 'churned and chewed' to give meaning to one's view of the world.

More importantly, education involves the inculcation or cultivation of attitudes and behaviours usually of the dominant cultural group of a given society. Thus for a child from a minority group (such as an Indonesian newcomer into Melbourne society) one of the first things she/he will learn is how to survive or be accepted by the immediate group with whom she/he has to interact. Such survival strategies may include things like:

- succumbing to bad or slang language
- dressing the same way
- mimicking culturally dissonant behaviours
- ensuring she/he is not always 'top of the class'
- avoid speaking his/her own cultural language at home, thus blocking out their original culture
- and many others

Furthermore the term education is not only perceived differently by different cultures but is also economically and politically driven. For example, the culture of Western Industrialised or High Technology societies would expect education to have high level inquiry skills that will lead to useful, and a greater choice of, well remunerated employment. Whilst the governments of such societies would expect education to lead to political lobbying by interest groups, these groups often determine the purpose, the name, the length and duration, the content, the processes and the quality of education and educational services.

Education is also defined as the acts of teaching and learning. However, it is more than just the imparting or receiving of information. Rather, it is a mixture of innate biological and social capacity to learn whilst teaching is dependent upon the availability, appropriateness and quality of both human and material resources. Both teaching and learning frequently require a touch of recalcitrant creativity.

Bahasa Indonesia and the Australian Education System

Some 27 years ago when I arrived in Melbourne, the skills of Australians in discriminating or differentiating individual South East Asian nations or ethnic groups was so poor that on the first day at school my younger brother and I were greeted by our peers with:

'Chinese, Japanese, money please'

dynamically expressed by their slanting eyes, faces and hair and gesticulating the request for monies. Having lived for some years in Malaysia prior to coming to Melbourne, and having experienced schooling amongst English children, we found this Australian chant somewhat peculiar, irritating but funny (in hindsight of course). According to Jamie Mackie (1994, pp.283) little has progressed from this time to the present in that Australian's perceptions, attitudes and knowledge of Indonesians and Indonesia have still not achieved the breadth and depth required to strengthen the relationship between the two countries. However, the same can also be probably said of Indonesians and their perceptions, attitudes and knowledge of Australia and Australians.

Apart from this minor incident in primary school, I have no other recollection of discriminatory antics or prejudice by my Western counterparts. I do believe however that it helps to speak English as fluently as possible. Australians are broadly tolerant people.

Others (that is other Indonesian children arriving post 1968) did experience difficulties but the level of difficulty appears related to their age group and personal development [see diagram 1].

Diagram 1: Levels of Difficulties experienced by newly arrived Indonesians

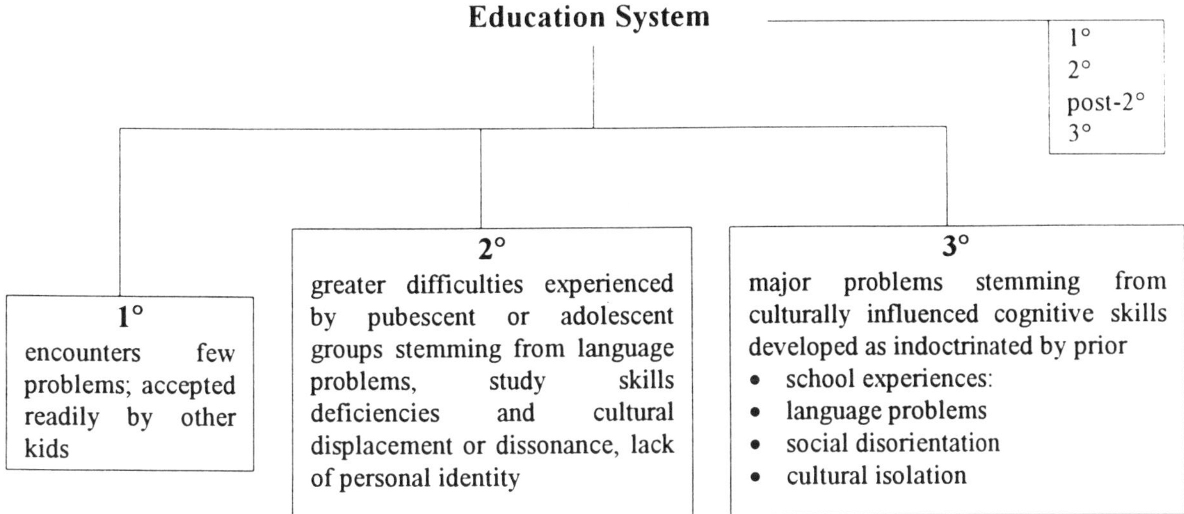

Many of the problems encountered by 1° and 2° students of Indonesian-Indonesian descent can be overcome by supportive, caring and disciplined family environments. That is, a family that is not only keen for their child to learn but a family that is keen to learn with/for their child.

[Anecdote]: As for my own experiences, not only did I have such a family, but that each sibling was able to teach and learn from each other. After all, the name 'Idrus' in Arabic means to learn, or to have knowledge. So, I really have no choice but to learn and consequently am still learning. Thus, it certainly is a lifelong endeavour.

Families are also critical in striking a balance between one's original culture, and cultural roots, and one's adopted culture. Such a balance is necessary for the personal development and identity of the child but also provides the child with a rationale for antecedent behaviours that are culturally derived. On the one hand one can be grateful for being bicultural but on the other hand, in some circumstances, being bicultural can have its pitfalls (particularly evident during early adolescence).

Some of the problems thus far mentioned are now reaching a critical point. that is, with the increasing number of Indonesian full-fee paying students and scholarship assisted students. Educational institutions have finally accepted that there are inadequate infrastructures to support the personal, cultural and learning needs of these students from whom institution and government are only too keen to accept monies. Voluntary organizations (community) ought not to be burdened with the expenses required to service such students but rather ought to be consulted with, and invited to collaborate in, the development of institutional infrastructures to cater for such students. Furthermore, the utilization of Indonesianists or experts in Bahasa Indonesia within any one institution to problem solve educational difficulties of Indonesian students (full fee paying or scholarship assisted) is neither appropriate nor recommended for obvious reasons. Ideally, the persons required to deal with such students' difficulties ought to have the following qualities:

(a) be 'bicultural' or have a practical experience (greater than 4 years in Indonesia, preferably within an educational context) of the Indonesian culture

(b) be a qualified educator (preferably in educational psychology) with recent experience in Australian institutions

(c) be cognisant with and comprehending of both the Indonesian and Australian government's policies and Australian institutions

(d) be aware of the existence of resources within the Indonesian community in Victoria.

Such services or infrastructures are necessary for the successful education experiences of these Indonesian students. After all, the major outcome of their educational experiences in Australia is not only the achievement of an academic award but more importantly the attainment of:

- resource networking; and
- sound knowledge base to act as credible ambassadors for Australia on their return to Indonesia and for years to follow.

As for the permanent residents in Victoria, the Victorian education system has served us all well. Within my peer group alone, I am proud to acknowledge the first wholly Victorian trained lawyer of full blooded Indonesian descent who is now a 'high flier' in the Office of Public Prosecutions. We also have a Principal Engineer at BHP; a Commander (Engineering Squadron, RAN-Submarine Corps); a well known journalist; an artist/singer; a senior academic and a researcher just to name a few. Other full-blooded Indonesian descendants have graduated in fields as diverse as the performing arts, engineering and law to areas such as the service industries including nursing, allied health, hospitality/hotel management and television direction.

Identifying New Directions

A. Reflecting upon history and experience.

Both the presence of Indonesians in Victoria and the development, establishment and expansion of the teaching of Bahasa Indonesia and Indonesian studies has to some extent, influenced the perceptions and attitudes of Australians towards Indonesians and Indonesia. However, an explicit National Strategy for making Indonesia better understood and thus to eliminate stereotypic and misleading views, has not yet been achieved.

B. Facing the future: Using the Australian education system to build bridges between Indonesia and Australia.

There are many of us today who are promoting not only Bahasa Indonesia but more importantly the cultures of Indonesia through non-language courses such as the Transcultural Midwifery Studies Course in which students are given opportunities to learn intensive Bahasa Indonesia and to experience 'lived culture' of midwifery practice in Indonesia through what is known as a preceptorship program.

The proliferation of such courses and the proliferation of Bahasa Indonesia at all levels of the education system must be monitored closely, particularly as there is evidence that-

(a) we have inadequate numbers of qualified LOTE teachers in BI;
(b) we have inadequate training of existing BI or Indonesia studies specialists in developing curricula;
(c) we have inadequate resources for the teaching of BI and Indonesian studies;
(d) we have undertaken little or negligible research that either substantiates or negates the efficiency and effectiveness of our BI courses;
(e) we do not have adequate peer review of our BI or IS teachers/academics.

Other reasons for close monitoring may be found by reading Jamie Mackie's paper in ESAU; Expanding Horizons: Australia and Indonesia into the 21st century, (1984).

Diagram 2: Shaping of Australian Attitudes Towards Indonesia and Indonesians

Indonesian Government	Australian Government	Indonesians in Victoria	Era	Outcomes
Fight for independent development of nations Beginning of New Order after 1963 confrontation	White Australia Policy Britain alliance partner in Indonesian push for independence	Colombo Plan students Radio Australia staff Academics development community organizations	1940s-1960s	Development of Indonesian sympathiser groups Beginning of BI development
New order needs -Repelita I, II, III, IV and V -growing population and growing need for education	Fraser government commitment to the expansion of assistance to developing nations in particular Indonesia.	AIDAB assisted scholarships	1970s-1980s	Expansion of BI and Indonesian studies East Timor incident cause setback to developments Growing recognition of Australia as providers of good education Increasing illegal immigrants
Growing economic growth Deregulation of trade and development	Economic boom followed by stock market crash Development of All National Agenda for MA Business Migration Keating government push for greater economic trade with Indonesia	Private school exchanges • growing academic, cultural exchanges • growing ethnic Chinese-Indonesians • growing single Indonesians under 21 years • greater 2° & 3° Ed students (FFP)	1980s-1990s	No more amnesty Growing size of Indonesian community Growing OSFF students Increase community understanding of Indonesians as a result of growing home stays and business

Apart from the contribution that Australia makes to the promotion of Indonesia, there are indeed some of us endeavouring to make Australia a tangible entity in Indonesia, by utilising the Australian education structures and implanting them in the Indonesian education system. For example, the offering of clinical skills courses in targeted existing Indonesian Universities and other health care teaching institutions. Other Australian university consortiums are developing other programs such as the development of on-site pre-university preparatory courses for students intending to undertake undergraduate programs in Australia. Some of us are implementing collaborative research endeavours and assisting in the development of management infrastructures of health care institutions. The Australian business sector is busy preparing to invest in Indonesia and to take advantage of the Indonesian government's recent deregulation package on trade and investment.

With a rapidly rising middle class, the demand and the need for effective and efficient healthcare and education will far surpass their availability. These are then opportunities for Australians and in particular for Australian-Indonesians. Thus, in summary, education certainly seems to be an appropriate strategy for bridging the gaps in Australia-Indonesia relations, particularly as the growth in the Indonesian middle class by the year 2000 will enhance the demand for more educational opportunities and for Australian educational institutions to recruit more full fee paying students. But be warned, this new middle class will be expecting more for their money, so if your course or program is not up to scratch you could lose this lucrative market to the USA. Advances in telecomunication may see the development of cross-institution teaching via satellite, without the inconvenience of uprooting oneself from one's home ground, and resolve the problem of inadequate teachers of BI. However, this will increase the need for student exchanges even from primary school level.

I could go on and on about the expanse of opportunities that exist in this bilateral relationship. However, be warned—at a 'flick' of change in government policies on either side, we could see the demise of what seems to be an upturn in good relations between Australia and Indonesia.

There will indeed be better understanding and better communication between the two communities as long as decision makers realise the importance and existence of exceptional resources available within the Indonesian communities throughout Australia, who have contributed to and will continue to contribute to good relations between the two countries.

Bibliography

Mackie, J. (1994). *In Each Other's Minds: Indonesia in Australian Minds*. In EAAU DFAT - Expanding Horizons: Australia & Indonesia into the 21st Century. AGPS, pp 283-302.

AIAWLS (1994). Papers presented on July and August 6th at Monash University. Unpublished papers.

References

Coopers and Lybrand Australia (1993). *Doing Business in Southeast Asia.*

Earl, G. (1993). *An Indonesian Visionary has Australia in his sights*. In Australian Financial Review, September 17.

Industries Assistance Commission. (1989). *Exploring Health and Education Services*. Discussion Paper No. 5, January. Canberra: AGPS.

JSCFAD&T. (1993). *Australia's relations with Indonesia. Canberra*: AGPS, pp.1-24; pp.25-33; Chaps. 9 &10.

Mackie, J. (1994). *In Each Other's Minds: Indonesia in Australian Minds*. In EAAU DFAT - Expanding Horizons: Australia & Indonesia into the 21st Century. AGPS, pp 283-302.

Porter, M. (1990). *The Competitive Advantage of Nations*. New York, USA: Fress Press.

World Bank. (1992). *Indonesia: Growth, Infrastructure and Human Resources.*

Business Connections

Peter Berry

Two types of business dominate trade with Indonesia, those that make a lot of money and those that lose a heck of a lot of money. Arguably, with more care and appropriate planning, the latter can be minimised.

Trade between Victoria and Indonesia has been booming. 1993 figures obtained from DEFAT show that Victoria's export to Indonesia was worth A$199 million. This makes up 11.7% of the A$1.13 billion Australian export to Indonesia selling food, pharmaceuticals, telecommunications, aerospace, mineral processing, education and plastics.

Victoria's largest export sales market in the region, by the way, is Singapore.

Many business connections were initiated by private enterprise. Among the Victorian business pioneers are *BHP, CRA* and *Ashton Mining* in mining and engineering, *John Holland* in construction, *ACI* in glass, *Pacific BBA* in plastic products, *Pacific Dunlop* in tyres, *GMH* and *Ford* in cars, *AMCOR* in packaging materials, *KPMG Peat Marwick* in consulting, especially in taxation agreements, *ANZ* and *National Bank* in banking, *Ansett* in airlines service, *Nufarm* in chemicals and *Monash University* in education services.

Relatively a late starter, the Victorian Government opened the Victorian Government Business Office in Jakarta only in June 1994, but ahead of New South Wales. Victoria is behind the Northern Territory, Western Australia, South Australia and Queensland when it comes to doing business with Indonesia. The Victorian government focusses its business in real estate and manufacturing, promoting the state as a safe place to invest in. It has also proposed to establish a sister state relationship with West Java. Actively assisting with technical advice are Melbourne Water, State Electricity Commission of Victoria and PMA.

The Commonwealth and Indonesian Governments organise regular meetings at the ministerial level and the Indonesian Consulate in Melbourne has excellent personnel who organise bi-monthly business neworking meetings at the Consulate. Indonesian trade and investment missions visit Victoria regularly. Those interested in starting business with Indonesia are encouraged to join the *Australia Indonesia Business Council* (AIBC) Victorian Branch.

Trade between Victoria and Indonesia, if conducted correctly, is bound to succeed, as the two have matching needs that complement each other. Victoria, for instance, has raw materials for Indonesia to manufacture its finished goods. While Victoria needs to contain labour costs, Indonesia has a huge labour pool. Victoria can provide the technological know-how to build Indonesia's much needed infrastructure. Victoria can provide the education to contribute to the development skills in Indonesia. The shortage of skilled service organizations in Indonesia can easily be supplemented by capacity in Victoria. The relatively affluent population in Victoria is an ideal target for Indonesia's tourism promotion.

When starting a business in Indonesia, there are several attitudinal aspects Australians will have to be aware of.

Personal relationships are very important. An Indonesian buyer prefers to buy from a personal friend rather than from a stranger, the quality of the item being less important.

It is not easy to go it alone. It would be wise to carefully select an Indonesian partner who knows the local scene. Middlemen are often necessary. They can often act as catalysts in realising successful ventures.

There are some common attitudinal stumbling blocks for Australians. Many people like to make money quickly but in Indonesia, you cannot rush this. Australians like written contracts drafted by their lawyers and other advisors. Indonesians are more inclined to rely on spoken agreements between trusted friends rather than lawyers, thus avoiding litigation. Indonesian decision making involves a lengthy process of reaching mutual agreement while Australians prefer decisions to be made at each stage of the process. Relationships between employer and employee are well-defined in Indonesia, while they are often less hierachal in Australia. Directness is welcome in Australia, but considered rude in Indonesia. Australians place importance on punctuality which can be frustrating when dealing with an Indonesian counterpart who operates on *jam karet* (flexible time). Business is conducted in an atmosphere of informality in Indonesia, while in Australia it is kept formal. Sometimes these gaps are difficult to breach.

Although it takes a lot more than just business acumen, doing business in Indonesia can be very rewarding, for both sides.

Summing Up

Janet Penny

Summarising what we have learned about the range of ideas and experiences described over these last three Tuesday evenings is not easy! But together the speakers have given us a picture of a special kind of migration. It is one of individuals, not groups; of freely taken decisions, not of flight; of romance rather than arranged marriages; of choice not of compulsion—and that includes the choice to return if it seems the best thing to do; and of a generally rich experience, not often one of terrible loneliness. This is a lively group of people who have fitted in with Australians remarkably well, yet maintained and shared their own—quite varied—sense of identity. They have done more than that. They have demonstrated a special Indonesian quality of adaptability.

The overwhelming impression of the early experiences reported on the first evening was one of bewilderment. What is expected of us? How do we reach out to understand one another? The puzzle was equally difficult for Indonesians and Australians alike.

The first individuals involved approached each other with curiosity, good will and great confusion about how to begin. There were advantages in this—there were no expectations of one another, and thus few prejudices. Since they did not at first intend to stay, the Indonesians arriving then posed no challenge to the racism of Australians, and Australians' natural sympathy for battlers was roused by Indonesia's revolution. Indonesians in their turn were grateful for sympathy and the help received. This has meant that throughout the next 45 years the individual contacts have built on this good will, constructing a bridge able to withstand the vicissitudes of relations between the governments.

Indonesian students left standing and looking at laundry coppers and piles of firewood, or Australians gasping for breath at the first taste of chilli can be likened to people crossing a river balanced on a log. Maret Soekotjo was able to re-create the feelings experienced by all those who came in those early days. According to him and also Rudy Munir, the Indonesians were received with extraordinary curiosity and warmth by many Australians and these young Indonesians were obviously good ambassadors. One can only try to imagine the difficulties involved in finding that basic stuff, rice, let alone learning to cook it with something tasty. Learning to do that had to be combined with numerous personal appearances and no doubt the eating of many lamb chops, not to mention plenty of hard professional work—all in English.

Rudy Munir and Mas Soekotjo described the close bonds that developed—between Australians and the first Indonesians who came, the students, officials, teachers and broadcasters—as they sought to understand those Australians and to present to the Australians the essence of Indonesia, that huge, complex, colourful but poor country, struggling to learn the skills of nationhood. Despite tremendous good will on all sides—even in some cases going so far as to marry—the Indonesians basically saw themselves as guests in those early years. To give themselves a base, these enterprising young people formed a range of organizations, to meet their social, religious and culinary needs. There would have been very few Muslims in Australia, so Rudy and others were brave enough to hire the Exhibition Buildings to inaugurate their first prayer meeting.

Hugh O'Neill gave us a picture of the other side of this early relationship, as he and his young family tackled similar problems on the other end of this early bridge. Living in the Indonesia of the 1950s clearly created a strong attachment, since he and many other volunteers have maintained a lifelong commitment to the relationship. When they returned to Australia their close bonds with the Indonesians who pioneered here have served as a strong link between individual friends and between the Indonesian and Australian communities.

As well as developing these links, the challenging task of explaining Indonesia's complex of languages and cultures was given to the first academics. Their success can be measured, as Rabin Hardjadibrata explained, not only in their impressive lists of publications, but in the growth of Indonesian studies programs, and the great number of Australians with knowledge of Indonesia and a keen interest in it. Pak Hardjadibrata himself has provided a key to the Indonesian language, making it possible for English speaking people to gain a more profound understanding of the people and the culture.

Those who were the most successful at this perilous log crossing have been the ones to stay with the relationship. If they were Indonesian, this meant to remain in Australia and work on that bridge: first a footbridge, based on the ties formed by these early arrivals, then by the 1960s something much more substantial, bolstered by a series of exchanges—diplomatic, artistic, tourist, business—and by more migrants.

It is much more difficult to categorise the people who arrived after the 1960s. Those who had come first were mostly well educated, middle class professionals and through the late 1960s they were joined by a few who had married Australians working in Indonesia and by some particularly adventurous young people—in some cases, one might even say footloose. At this point, the Australians ended their racially restrictive immigration policy and by the mid 1970s Indonesia's prosperity made it possible for greater numbers of individuals—without government sponsorship—to make the trip. Their educational qualifications varied widely—just over half who came in the 1970s were men—they did not come to fill special needs, but they took their chances with all other migrants, not altogether sure they wanted to stay. At the same time Australians took to travelling to Asia in greater numbers. Our bridge had become quite a highway.

This free flow was restricted after 1978, with further changes in Australian policy. This time the restrictions were not concerned with race, but rather with qualifications that would fill Australian needs. Indonesians continued to arrive, many were sent home and the community changed again.

The speakers on the second evening looked at ways in which the resident Indonesians, once established, were able—even eager—to reach out into the wider Victorian community. Dr Tuti Gunawan described the transition in the community which took place after the mid-1970s in response to these changes. The close knit group living here had formed associations to fill the gaps of extended family and networks of 'konneksi' they had left in Indonesia—and also to help newcomers to settle. Suddenly the organizations formed for these purposes—*Ikawiria*, PPI, the AIA—were faced with a completely new kind of community. The dislocations in the existing groups—and the formation of new ones, such as Perwira, with its emphasis on maintaining strong and loyal links with Indonesia—were in part a response to this challenge. Not only were new people, with different backgrounds and interests arriving but also those who had remained in Australia were becoming integrated and developing a new relationship with both Australia and Indonesia, believing it was feasible to be attached to both countries. In the discussions which followed the talks on the second evening, it became evident just how complicated this can be, when not only does one's attachment to Australia change over time, but Indonesia itself changes. The migrants recognise that there are difficulties in adapting at such a distance to those changes. Thus, last week, we were able to see how the community groups worked to consolidate their positions and also to reach out to the wider community of Australians.

Both Dr Tuti Gunanwan and Hilary Da Costa described the ways the organizations have done this; not only have they tried to serve the needs of those living here, but they also became involved, both as individuals and as such groups, in Australian cultural affairs. They have done this through official channels connected with the policy of multiculturalism, by radio broadcasts and by joining others to form pressure groups resisting anti-Asian and anti-immigration attitudes.

Hilary told us how the AIA, an organization specifically aimed at promoting good relations has responded to changes. There have been times when interest and membership has waxed and waned, partly in response to the relationship between the countries. The AIA in particular has helped to develop links between the people interested in both countries, with its consistent language teaching program and with a range of social and educational occasions, such as this one.

Poedijono seems to have formed a kind of one-man movement! He has displayed that special Indonesian talent for adaptability, in using the resources at hand (sometimes the only resources were hands) to combine elements of various forms and styles to create a new synthesis of Indonesian arts and Australian arts in ways that convey Indonesian ideas to Australian audiences. A particular point needs to be made here: most of the Indonesians who have come here are from cities, and most live in Australian cities, therefore this bridge has mainly been an urban to urban one. Poedijono has, on the other hand, taken his enthusiasm—one might even say his missionary zeal—to the Australian countryside and one can be sure he has left a lasting impression.

In the third set of lectures the speakers pointed out some directions that this relationship is likely to take in the future, with increasing family links, increasing educational exchanges and with the development of trade between Indonesia and Australia.

An important element in the developing links involves Indonesian-Australian marrriages and to amplify that experience, Ailsa Thompson and her husband Zainud'din provided an entertaining and illuminating example. Cross-cultural involvement does not go much deeper than that experienced in a marriage, proved by the fact that their speeches were alternating and interwoven as their lives between two countries have been. Their approach has been creative since, in feeling free to cast aside expected patterns of family life, they have built on the material, spiritual and intellectual strength available from both cultures.

Dr Karen Kartomi, as the product of another mixed marriage, has become a positive example of what happens when the 'multi' is really 'cultural'. She has lived in a house full of music and taken the opportunity to bring the cultures together intellectually. She has managed to meld everything—the beauty of both races, the languages and music of both cultures, the teaching of language and music.

Zulfikar Alimuddin seems, as a current engineering student, to link the experiences of the first bridge builders with the present ones. He brings to his study of technology a sophisticated desire to learn everything he can while studying here about the social infrastructures that underpin Western society and technology. He demonstrates great enthusiasm for developing organizational skills and functional networks between two countries and most significantly, a broad perception of not only Australian values but of Indonesian ones as well.

It was clear from Lanita Idrus that not all students are as able to take full advantage of their chance to study in Australia as is Zulfikar Alimuddin. She takes Australian educational institutions to task, pointing out the missed opportunity for enabling students from Indonesia to take full advantage of the chance not only to succeed in their course of study, but also to learn the best of Western culture. She makes it clear that by missing this chance Australia is likely to be the loser in the long run, as the best—and subsequently the most influential—students will prefer to attend German or American institutions. She makes clear recommendations for Australian tertiary institutions to develop effective advisory and infrastructure systems to take full advantage of this opportunity.

Finally, Peter Berry from Price Waterhouse was able to give some brief practical examples of developing and shared economic developments. He touched on approaches used by companies such as his own when preparing Australian business people for working in the Indonesian environment. It is essential to evaluate the best way to function in the business environment, if business relations and trade are to succeed and play thir role in strengthening the links between the two countries in general, and Victoria and Indonesia in particular.

Before closing it is worth emphasising that Indonesia has had a long history of merging cultures. Joining an already rich and complex cultural mix, there was first Hinduism, Buddhism and other elements of Indian culture; then Islam and Middle Eastern idealogical systems; then Christianity and Western culture. The Indonesians' particular ability to choose from each of these cultures that which suits them best and combine them to form a national identity, has utilised and developed a special talent. They, more than most people, are able to evaluate what a certain culture has to offer, choose that which best fits their existing cultural life and adopt the best parts. This has made the Indonesian adjustment to life in Australia particularly successful.

Finally—returning to that bridge—the traffic between the two sides is becoming a movement between two peoples sharing increasing similarities. A strong bridge will enable the traffic to move smoothly in both directions. We are grateful to those who began the construction of this bridge, with little awareness of its potential and without much of a structure to support them. Because of their labours, the present community can continue to strengthen and extend the bridge. We who have been able to participate in this lecture series have been fortunate to travel on it.